THE SPIRITUAL JOURNEY OF
George Washington

Other Books by Janice T. Connell

Queen of the Cosmos
The Visions of the Children
Triumph of the Immaculate Heart
Angel Power
Meetings with Mary
Praying with Mary
Prayer Power
Queen of Angels

THE SPIRITUAL JOURNEY OF
George Washington

JANICE T. CONNELL

Hatherleigh Press

New York   London

Hatherleigh Press
5-22 46th Avenue
Long Island City, NY 11101
www.hatherleighpress.com

Library of Congress Cataloging-in-Publication Data

Connell, Janice T.
  The spiritual journey of George Washington / Janice T. Connell.
      p. cm.
  Includes bibliographical references.
  ISBN 978-1-57826-248-9
 1. Washington, George, 1732-1799--Religion. 2. Washington, George, 1732-1799--Philosophy. 3. Presidents--United States--Biography. I. Title.
  E312.17.C665 2007
  973.4'1092--dc22

                                    2007016606

ISBN 978-1-57826-248-9
The Spiritual Journey of George Washington is available for bulk purchase, special promotions, and premiums. For information on reselling and special purchase opportunities, call 1-800-528-2550 and ask for the Special Sales Manager.

Interior design by Tai Blanche
Cover design by Deborah Miller

10 9 8 7 6 5 4 3 2
Printed in the United States

Dedication

*T*his book is dedicated to George Washington and all brave patriots, living, deceased, yet to be born, who in any way lend their hearts, skills, strength, prayers to protect and defend the ideals of the United States of America. May such wisdom bring peaceful life, liberty and the continued pursuit of happiness.

* * *

There are no coincidences.
It is not by accident that you have this book.

Contents

Cover Image by Arnold Friberg

Foreword

"[I]t is a point conceded that America, under an efficient government, will be the most favorable Country of any in the world for persons of industry and frugality, possessed of a moderate capital, to inhabit. It is also believed, that it will not be less advantageous to the happiness of the lowest class of people because of the equal distribution of property, the great plenitude of unoccupied lands, and the facility of procuring the means of substance."
—George Washington[1]

George Washington's deeds are his greatest legacy. Three significant realities in his life propelled him to immortality. First, he was born into rather ordinary circumstances. Secondly, he used the opportunities life presented him to feed the hungry, give drink to the thirsty, clothe and shelter the needy, care for the imprisoned, visit the sick, bury the dead, admonish, instruct, counsel, forgive and pray for others. Thirdly, and undoubtedly the most significant, he never allowed success or failure to corrupt him.

As you examine the evidence in this small book, treasure the stories that allow Washington's character to shine through the prism of time. You will find that for George Washington who was born into a Christian family, lived as a practicing Anglican/Episcopalian Mason and circumstantially died in the Catholic faith, patriotism meant private, personal commitment to the great God of Abraham—"our

Father who art in Heaven,"—expressed through loving deeds for humanity. After you weigh the enclosed expert testimony and savor examples of Washington's choices in the framework of his life, take the next step. Make a decision. Go forth and use this information. There are no lost opportunities for true patriots.

Chronology

February 22, 1732: Birth of George Washington in British colony of Virginia

1752: Appointed Major of Virginia Militia

1753: Military duty in Ohio Valley, Pennsylvania

1754–1763: French and Indian War

1754: Washington acts as Aide to British General Edward Braddock at battle for Fort Duquesne

1755–1758: Washington serves as Commander in Chief of Virginia Military forces

1758–1775: Member of Virginia House of Burgess

January 6, 1759: Wedding of George Washington and Martha Dandridge Custis

1765: British Parliament passes the Stamp Act

1773: December "Boston Tea Party"

1774: Washington attends first Continental Congress

1775: Washington elected General and Commander in Chief of the Continental Forces

July 4, 1776: Declaration of Independence

Winter 1777–1778: Valley Forge

October, 1781: Defeat of British General Charles Cornwallis at Yorktown, Virginia

1787: General George Washington elected President of the Constitutional Convention, in Philadelphia

June, 1788: United States Constitution ratified

February 4, 1789: George Washington unanimously elected first President of the United States

February 13, 1793: Washington reelected President for second term

December 1797: Washington retires to Mount Vernon

December 14, 1799: George Washington dies at Mount Vernon

Introduction

My first wish is to see this plague to mankind, war, banished from the earth.
—George Washington

merican History is a comfort to Americans for it teaches that God, "a Kind Providence"[2] brings good out of evil. His mercy is greater than all His works.[3] George Washington knew the "All Wise and Most Gracious Providence"[4] well. He believed the Gates of Paradise are wide and the Blood of the Lamb has obtained entry for all redeemed, willing children of the Father.[5] Washington recognized that every man rises and falls on the choices he makes every moment. Like Abraham and Moses, Washington pleaded with God, whom he referred to as "That Being in whose hands are all of human events,"[6] "That Being who sees, foresees, and directs all things,"[7] (and especially at Valley Forge[8]) "That Being who is powerful to save, and in whose hands is the fate of nations."[9] Throughout his life, Washington appealed to this God of mercy with loud cries. He conquered in the name of the "All Wise and all Powerful Director of Human Events",[10] led in His ways, "the Lord and Giver of All Victory,"[11] and died in His bosom, the "Pure and Benign Light of Revelation."[12]

Washington was not a stranger to sorrow, cold, hunger, persecution, violence or terrorism. George Washington's great accomplishment was to face misfortune and conquer it; he achieved victory by discipline, commitment, prayer and the graced ability to bend his will under the yoke of "a Kind Providence." He was a stoic who triumphed over suffering with ascetic heroism.

Consider the stress General Washington endured, the courage and spiritual confidence he mustered with his pitiful army and the victory he and his men achieved against all odds:

> "...[I]t will not be believed that such a force as Great Britain has employed for eight years in Country could be baffled...by numbers infinitely less, composed of Men oftentimes half starved; always in Rags, without pay, and experiencing, at times, every species of distress which human nature is capable of undergoing."[13]

More than two hundred years after his death, his deeds, letters and hand-written diaries continue to disclose the depths of George Washington, sincerely the most spiritually enlightened and courageous man among the best of the Founding Fathers. Contemporary thinkers are studying the life and works of the first President of the United States with wisdom and renewed vigor. Celebrated biographer Joseph J. Ellis calls George Washington "...the most ambitious, determined and patient personality...*primus enter pares*...the Foundingist of the Founding Fathers."[14] Eminent scholar Michael Novak, writing with his daughter Jana observes: "Washington instructed his men—and later the whole nation—to pray for God's continuing interventions on behalf of the preservation and the prospering of freedom on earth.... He prayed to his God as the same God to whom the ancient Israelites had prayed, and as the same to whom Jesus addressed the Lord's Prayer: Our Father who art in Heaven...give us this day our daily bread...and deliver us from evil...."[15] Distinguished biographer David McCullough, in his masterful *1776*, quotes a young officer who served under General Washington at the Battle of Princeton; an eyewitness account of the greatness of the Commander-in-Chief under attack. "I shall never forget what I felt....when I saw him brave all the dangers of the field and his important life hanging as it were by a single hair with a thousand deaths flying around him."[16]

George Washington, man of destiny, started his career young. When he was twenty-one years old, the Virginia officer led a small battalion of about 140 troops to protect the western lands of the English crown.[17] They traveled over the Blue Ridge and Allegheny Mountains from Williamsburg into what was called "the Ohio Country" and on to what is now Erie, Pennsylvania, to a French outpost at Presque Isle. There, the enthusiastic Washington delivered what eventually proved to be the verbal shot that began the French and Indian War; the following message from his Colonial Governor, Robert Dinwiddie on behalf of His Britannic Majesty, King George I.

"The Lands upon the river Ohio, in the Western Parts of the Colony of Virginia, are so notoriously known to be the Property of the Crown of Great

Britain, that it is a matter of equal Concern & Surprise to me [Governor Dinwiddie] to hear that a Body of French Forces are erecting Fortresses, and making Settlements upon the River within his Majesty's dominions."[18]

Of course, trained-to-be-gracious French officers received young George Washington at their fort with due courtesy, and did nothing with his edict from the Colonial Governor of Virginia. They, after all, represented the King of France.

At twenty-two, Captain Washington was dispatched with his regiment to Fort Duquesne (now Pittsburgh, Pennsylvania) to protect the western lands. Young Washington achieved a small victory at Jumonville, in the spring of 1754, but not without cost to the sensitivities of his soul. He reported a seminal war incident by his Indian guides which happened so quickly he was unable to intervene:

"...5 or 6 Indians had chosen to knock the poor, wounded [French prisoners of war] in the head, and bereiv'd them of their scalps."[19]

That would not happen again under his watch.

As a young surveyor and youthful military leader in the Ohio Valley, Washington witnessed terrorism unleashed upon American colonists who were "...exposed to the tortures and killings in which the Indians habitually indulged themselves..."[20] He wrote of his personal experience on the frontier:

" ...[F]ive hundred Indians have it more in their power to annoy the inhabitants, than ten times their number of regulars. For besides the advantageous way they have of fighting in the woods, their cunning and craft are not to be equaled, neither their activity and indefatigable sufferings. They prowl about like wolves, and, like them, do their mischief by stealth. They depend upon their dexterity in hunting and upon the cattle of the inhabitants for provisions."[21]

He wrote from the frontier to Governor Dinwiddie on April 22, 1756:

"The supplicating tears of the women, and moving petitions from the men, melt me into such deadly sorrow, that I solemnly declare, if I know my own mind, I could offer myself a willing sacrifice to the butchering enemy, provided that would contribute to the people's ease."[22]

It is improbable that youthful George Washington realized at the time he wrote those plaintiff words to his superior he was in fact identifying his own destiny. George Washington would indeed go on to offer himself a willing sacrifice to many a butchering enemy for the people he served.

By the mid 1700's, Washington's adventures on the frontier, published as *The Journals of Major George Washington*, thrilled readers in the colonies and as far away as England and Scotland. The young explorer soldier wrote of treacherous mountain ranges, untamed forests, raging rivers and uncivilized natives quite willing to torture and destroy unsuspecting white settlers, and even one another.

Washington's legend grew out of his pen, dipped in the blood of the mighty frontier, reporting incidents, geography and military stealth that Europeans and most colonists could barely imagine. Few would know much about the heights and depths of George Washington, the man for all ages, but for his pen. Washington told about the reality he saw. Who can dispute the horrors and hardship he described, of abandoning worn out, dying horses and heading onward on foot through blinding snow to the Indian village known as "Murdering Town"? And what of the two decaying, scalped adults, a man and a woman, and five scalped children he discovered, being eaten by starving dogs on the banks of the Monongahela River?[23]

Washington's journal also introduced readers to a mighty ally-to-be, turn coat, and sometimes friend. Half King, the Seneca Chief known to his tribe as Tanacharison, was the diplomatic representative of the Iroquois Confederation (the Six Nations) headquartered in Onondaga, New York. It seems those particular Indians had long memories. Half King called George Washington the "Devourer of Villages," "Conotocarius" in Indian parlance, the very name the tribe had given to George Washington's great-grandfather, John Washington, a hundred years or so ago.[24] Young Washington quickly determined that European colonists were considered temporary interlopers by Native American inhabitants who held deep-set religious claims to the American continent. Washington quoted Half King:

"Both you [the French settlers] and the English are white. We live in a Country between. Therefore the Land does not belong either to one or the other; but the Great Being above allow'd it to be a Place of Residence for us."[25]

Washington's youthful experiences on the frontier exposed him to religious beliefs and superstitions which conflicted with his own deeply cultivated Biblical knowledge, and long standing family traditions rooted in the Anglican faith. Yet, the young man of destiny resonated with the sincerity and skills of those he met in the wilderness. George Washington was on a searing search for ultimate truth and wisdom that would lead to abundance, prosperity and happiness. Ostensibly, they were too. Indians on the frontier taught Washington much, not the least of which was humility. He quickly learned the danger of self-centered religious practices that legitimize human brutality. As a consequence, Washington steadfastly separated his personal religious convictions from his legitimate claims of authority over others.

Washington was a man of prayer. Undoubtedly, his spirituality was the result of family traditions, culture, lived experiences and self-taught studies. George Washington, a kind man, practiced what he believed, not by words, but by heroic deeds that enriched and ennobled those he served. Therein lies his greatness. Shortly before the Declaration of Independence became a reality, realistic Washington wrote to John Adams on April 15, 1776:

"We have nothing, my Dear Sir, to depend upon but the protection of a Kind Providence and unanimity among ourselves."[26]

George Washington, the spiritual man, refused to comingle his Christian linguistic understanding of God with his secular office when he wrote to Adams of "Kind Providence," even though Adams was of an outspoken Christian background. One might rightfully ask the source of Washington's knowledge of Providence as "kind." Here we begin to fathom the depths of Washington's highly tested, profoundly private Christian faith. Who is kinder than Jesus Christ saying from His cross of execution: "Forgive them Father. They know not what they do."? Throughout his life of service to his country, George Washington would continue to identify the great God of Abraham, "our Father who art in Heaven", as "Kind Providence," "All Wise and Most Gracious Providence." He would name God in his writings, speeches and statements with upwards of 100 titles, each revealing his terribly private Christ-filled depths.

Obviously, "Kind Providence," the "Supreme Dispenser of Every Good," heard Washington's humble, often desperate prayers, tested him mightily and rewarded his constituency generously. Liberty steeped in just law came to life in America, but at a price each subsequent generation of Americans is called upon to honor.

Against seemingly insurmountable odds, George Washington valiantly led America into freedom's merciful light. His deeds, diaries and letters reveal General George Washington, first and only unanimously elected President of the United States burning with faith in the goodness of Divine Providence and the sibling relationship of the earth's people. That supernatural faith in action ignited a fire which warmed the hearts of Native Americans, colonists, Europeans, and even Barbary pirates, eventually spreading the American ideal to the entire world. Washington's dream was that people of every race, culture and religion bloom side by side in America as gently as spring breezes nurture flowers and trees and seas and deserts. Americans are the beneficiaries of George Washington's wisdom: the legislative, executive and judicial branches of the U.S. government bear legal and moral imperatives to maintain it.

Washington's vision of the Separation of Church and State is sewn into the fabric of American life, and codified by the First Amendment. The "Church" remains an institution for "believers to congregate and worship in the private sphere."[27] The "State" on the contrary, is a "collective milieu of civic, political and legal arrangements in which we live while in the Public Square. The Church is private religion— be it Evangelical or mainline Protestantism, conservative or liberal Catholicism, Orthodox, Reform or Conservative Judaism, or any variant of Islam, Buddhism, Hinduism and so on. The specific beliefs, practices and positions of any faith are protected from government interference by the First Amendment, which mandates religious freedom."[28]

George Washington's example, his writings, his very demeanor—subtle though it was, brought forth the platform upon which "public religion" (as opposed to "private religion") rests. Through all known relics of George Washington's leadership, one finds the underlying foundation for "public religion": a "spirit of kindness to others… a generous moral disposition, and rituals acknowledging a dependence on divine providence."[29] Thanksgiving Day, a national holiday instituted by George Washington, is just one example of "public religion."

Washington hoped that the American continent, a great land of opportunity, would play a unique spiritual role in the on-going development of the human race. His personal faith in the kindness and mercy of God, as revealed in Jesus Christ, supported his national public faith which called for citizens to experience the American paradigm of liberty steeped in just law. Washington did not act alone. His accomplishments and writings disclose that "a Kind Providence," the "Wise Disposer of all Events"[30] was in him, around him and always with him.

This small, abbreviated narrative of certain segments of George Washington's life is offered as a resource for those everywhere who seek peace among nations, prosperity, and global fellowship rooted in meritorious decency. May it illumine more brightly the living spirit of American liberty. The United States, in spite of and perhaps because of fierce challenges, remains one nation under God, the "Lord and Ruler of Nations,"[31] with liberty and justice for all. The nation's freedom will endure only as long as its citizens sustain it. America's system of government is the child of wisdom and the ward of vigilance. George Washington's tested supernatural faith in God's "Superintending Power"[32] is his finest bequest. His wisdom that reminds us of "Kind Providence," the "Supreme Ruler of the Universe"[33] offers a unique opportunity for people to work together to preserve the ideal of

"America the Beautiful." George Washington's spiritual lega-cy is kindly light from the "Great Author of Every Public and Private Good."[34]

PART ONE

In the Beginning

Young George Washington learned from the cradle that the Bible was the source of his solace; the roadmap for his spiritual, political, social and financial life. But experience was his mentor.

CHAPTER ONE

Washington's Early Years

*"Without virtue and without integrity, the finest talents
and the most brilliant accomplishments can never gain the
respect or conciliate the esteem of the truly valuable part
of mankind."*[35]
—George Washington

*G*eorge Washington's forebears were among the early settlers of Virginia; they descended from an English shipmaster, John Washington, who immigrated to Virginia about 1658. John had left England to escape shame and financial hardship flowing from religious persecution. His goal was to seek peaceful prosperity in commerce.

John Washington's father had been an ordained Puritan Minister, the Reverend Lawrence Washington of Purleigh, England. Fellow Puritans in England had arbitrarily deprived him of his livelihood, condemning him for practicing Anglican Catholicism. His congregation accused him of "drunkenness" because he continued to say Mass at a time when such rituals were not appreciated.[36] Though history is silent about details of Reverend Washington's life, the shame of the punishment wrought upon the family was intolerable for young John and he fled to Virginia to escape the social and financial harshness that flowed from its bitterness.

Youthful John Washington found Virginia's soil fertile and bountiful. The climate was mild and the land was beautiful. Farming was healthful and profitable for him. Before long his discipline and industriousness placed him among Virginia's landed gentility. His posterity would rank among the first families in the colony.

Religious freedom, paired with financial opportunity, gave John Washington powerful incentives to hold fast to his family spiritual traditions. Because of his influence, the beliefs, manners and culture of John's posterity in Virginia remained rooted in English Puritanism steeped in Anglican Catholicism.

Puritans in the colonies were a sect of English Calvinists struggling to purify the Church of England of excesses they thought were nonconforming to the New Testament and early Christian practice. The strictest Puritans, largely concentrated in New England, believed in the union of Church and State. They desired to produce a Christian society conformed to Sacred Scripture as they understood it.[37] They were severe and intolerant of non-conformists. Puritanism as practiced by George Washington's forbears in Virginia, however, was more moderate and largely a reaction to the frivolity, extravagance and moral corruption that pervaded the English Court, clergy and upper classes.[38]

In the colonies, the Church of England was known as the Anglican (Latin for "English") Church. In the words of

Professor David L. Holmes: "Throughout the colonial period, the Church of England was the established Church of Colonial Virginia. Colonial Virginians were born into the Anglican faith … The Virginia General Assembly legislated for the established Church, supported it through taxation, and protected it against competition."[39] Anglicanism in George Washington's day was essentially a middle way between lax Roman Catholicism and Eastern Orthodoxy on the one hand, and harsh English Calvinism on the other. The Anglican Church was more Catholic than Protestant, but substantially more Protestant than Rome or Constantinople. "It claimed to be a unique synthesis of Catholicism and Protestantism."[40] Anglicanism attempted to fuse the best of ancient Christianity with the sensitivities of English desires.

George Washington's family belonged to the Anglican Church; he was born into Anglicanism, lived his life as a practicing member, and was buried with the full rituals of the Anglican Church. The Washingtons, along with others similarly situated in Virginia, embraced the Thirty-nine Articles of Religion of the Anglican faith. However, they did away with the hierarchical strata of clergy above the rank of parish priest.[41] George Washington descended from ancestors who strongly believed "life is empty without religion…. [T]he tree of knowledge is barren unless rooted in love….[L]earning purchased at the expense of living is a sorry bargain."[42] There was ample time for Bible study in most Virginia family homes. The Washington family library contained theology books that chronicled God's temporal as well as spiritual rewards and punishments for behavior and each subsequent generation studied these works.

George Washington, born on February 22, 1732, was the eldest of six children of Augustine Washington and his second wife, Mary Ball. Augustine, a widower when he married Mary, was a third generation Virginian and the grandson of John Washington. Augustine was not a rich man, but his holdings were substantial; he worked hard and enjoyed moderate wealth. George, his third son and first child with Mary, was quite interesting to his father and older brothers. Augustine "paid shrewd attention to him, ensuring that he would grow up into a good, smart and honest man."[43] Desiring to teach George to honor his Creator by praising the works of His Hand, he taught his son that God is active in the world. Furthermore, he taught young George that God can be recognized by prayer and awareness of the Creator's presence in all that lives. An apocryphal story by Parson Mason Locke Weems survives that illumines Augustine's strategy to teach his young son George about the Fatherhood of God.

According to Parson Weems, young George's devout father helped him plant cabbage seeds in a plot near their house in a pattern spelling out G-E-O-R-G-E. He insisted George carefully tend and water the plot. Augustine was overjoyed at his child's delight with the cabbage patch when at last his name, G E O R G E, emerged from the ground. "How did that happen?" the much amazed boy asked. "What do you think?" his father asked him. Of course, George had no answer. Pointing to the cabbage patch, his father said: "This is a great thing, an important thing, a vital thing…I want you to understand, my son, that I am introducing you to your *true* father, the source and sustenance of all life, even yours."[44]

George Washington's mother, destined to be a woman of sorrow, was an orphan when she married his father. Mary Washington was of moderate height, rounded figure and pleasant voice.[45] A devout, demanding and strict woman, she would remain a challenge to her famous son during her entire life. Young George learned from the cradle that the Bible was the source of his solace; the roadmap for his spiritual, political, social and financial life. But experience was his mentor. In his region, there were strict laws against breaking the Sabbath, contempt of the Bible, disrespect for its teachings, and speaking against ordained ministers. Idleness, betting, drunkenness and intemperance in attire were forbidden. Righteousness, loyalty and devotion to family were required.

George Washington's father was familiar with suffering and hardship. He worked long hours to support his large, needy family. He directed a plantation, looked after his other farms and supervised an iron furnace he owned thirty miles distant from his residence. Augustine was no stranger to manual labor and was often away from home attending to his business interests. Before George was three years old, he stood with his father at the burial of his half-sister, Jane.

When George was six, Lawrence, his twenty-year-old half-brother, left Appleby, his father's school in England, and returned to Virginia to help Augustine. Unwell and busy with many occupations, Augustine entrusted Lawrence with partial management of the plantation in order to train him in agriculture. Lawrence loved his young half-brother George and inspired him with his tales and feats. George thrived under the tutelage of his fascinating elder brother whom he greatly admired. Elegant, filled with charm, grace and manners, Lawrence would always be George's hero.

On June 17, 1740, Governor William Gooch of Virginia commissioned Lawrence one of only four military leaders for the entire colony of Virginia, insuring that he would see the forts of Cartagena, hear war cannons and watch battles. George delighted in Lawrence's cultured behavior, athletic prowess, military skills and manly stories about life beyond Virginia.

Tragedy struck again when George was 11. His father died suddenly, leaving the financial position of his widow and children ambiguous. Lawrence probated his father's will; the estate included more than ten thousand acres, at least forty-nine slaves and an interest in the iron furnace. Young George inherited some real estate and ten slaves. However, his father had directed that the estates of his children by Mary Ball remain in their mother's guardianship during their minority. Thus, George's inheritance was not valuable. This fact would require him to acquire keen business skills and develop extraordinary qualities of leadership.

From his modest beginnings, self-made George Washington would become the most admired of leaders. Washington's professional, social and political acumen was brilliant in its sheer achievement. He honestly acquired huge real estate holdings; his business ventures were vast. Though he acquired a fortune, he shared it and bequeathed it away. He set official precedents for all Presidents of the United States to follow and for all Commanders in Chief of the Armed Forces, yet relinquished his lofty positions with graceful valor. He owned slaves in Virginia and, contrary to the laws of the State, gave them de facto citizenship at Mount Vernon, educated them and arranged for their freedom and upkeep when he was no longer alive to protect them. George Washington was formed by life's experiences, coincidences, hardships and serendipities. Self- taught George Washington acquired a library of 700 books, many of which he assiduously studied.[46] In his lifetime, he was awarded an honorary LL.D from Harvard University in 1776, Yale University, 1781, University of Pennsylvania, 1783, Washington College (Maryland) 1789, Brown University, 1790. He who would match wits with the most erudite of men, possessing the finest education of the times, had only a school boy's formal education.

George Washington carried within himself an almost perfect balance of faith, intellectual prowess and practical, hands-on experience. Those attributes ennobled the Founding Father of the United States; he was the driving force that carved out of the hard rock of humanity a lasting system of government for the people and by the people.

CHAPTER TWO

The Rules of Civility

"Labor to keep alive in your breast that little spark of celestial fire called conscience."[47]
—George Washington

*G*eorge Washington enthusiastically embraced life's lessons. In 1745, when he was thirteen years old, young George transcribed *The Rules of Civility and Decent Behavior in Company and Conversation* in colonial shorthand in his school workbook.[48] These *Rules of Civility* were taught to Washington during his first year of study with Reverend James Marye, a French Jesuit turned Anglican priest and rector of St. George's Church in Fredericksburg.[49] Reverend Marye also taught Washington mathematics, Latin and deportment. School boy George was required to learn the *Rules of Civility* by heart. They were the code of civil, social and cultural behavior for respectable gentlemen of his times. Washington accomplished his lessons perfectly.

The history of those *Rules of Civility* dates from the 1590s. French Jesuit priests distilled the spiritual exercises of their Spanish founder, Ignatius of Loyola, and incorporated them with rules of deportment for European nobility known as "110 Rules for Young Gentlemen."[50] Washington's handwritten copy of these *Rules* in his personal notebook is now in the Library of Congress.[51]

The *Rules of Civility* that governed Washington's code of behavior convey Ignatian discipline designed to form the authentic spiritual man. They allow adherents exquisite awareness that man is God's servant, on earth to honor his fellow man as he would like to be honored in everyday life, living not for self, but for the good of all. *The Rules of Civility* were so gentlemanly that they even included regulations concerning suitable table manners and proper conversation.

That Washington appropriated the *Rules of Civility* into his personality and social-political behavior is evident throughout his remaining life. Consider what Abigail Adams, wife of George Washington's vice president, John Adams, said of the first president of the United States:

"No man ever lived, more deservedly beloved and Respected. The praise and I may say adulation which followed his administration for several years, never made him forget that he was a Man, subject to the weakness and frailty attached to human nature. He never grew giddy, but ever maintained a modest diffidence of his own talents, and if that was an error, it was of the amiable and engaging kind... Possesst of power, possesst of an extensive influence, he never used it but for the benefit of his Country....When assailed by faction, when reviled by Party, he suffered with dignity, and retired from his exalted station with a Character which malice would not wound, nor envy tarnish. If we look through the whole tenor of his Life, History will not produce to us a Parallel."[52]

Such praise finds origin in Washington's properly formed conscience and refined spiritual nature.

The Rules of Civility were tools he used to achieve excellence in personal conduct. They shine brightly as cardinal principles of Washington's leadership. An excerpted version of the *Rules of Civility* in somewhat modernized English usage follows.

The Rules of Civility

Let all actions performed in public show some sign of respectful sentiment to the entire company.

When in the presence of others, refrain from touching any part of the body that is not usually within view. The hands and feet are ordinarily visible. In order to form the habit in this point of etiquette, practice it when you are with intimate friends.

Show nothing to your companion that may grieve him, since that might provoke a misunderstanding.

Do not seek amusement by singing to yourself, unless you are beyond the hearing of others; do not tap out the beat of a drum with your hands or feet.

Whenever you cough or sneeze, if you can control these natural efforts, do not sound off so highly or loudly. Do not heave sighs so noisily that others hear. When you yawn, refrain from any sound. Try to avoid yawning altogether when you are in company or engaged in conversation for it is a clear sign of certain weariness with those about you. If you cannot stop from yawning, avoid gaping widely and refrain from speaking while doing. Also, press at your mouth adroitly or turn a little away from the company.

It is an affront and an impertinence to doze while everyone is engaged in conversation, to be seated while the rest stand, or to walk on while others pause, or to speak when you should be silent or listen.

It is not becoming to leave your room while your bed is in disorder, or to dress or undress in the presence of others, or to leave your bedroom half-dressed, half-groomed, or to remain standing in your chamber or at your desk in immodest attire. And although you may have servants to make your bed; nevertheless, take care when you go out of your chamber not to leave your bed uncovered.

It is bad manners in sports, recreation, and at the fireside, to make a new-comer wait very long for a place. Guard against becoming overheated in temperament; don't let excitements carry you away. (Equates excitement with loud speech.)

Do not spit in the fire [place], nor stoop low before it. Neither put your hands into the flames to warm them, nor set your feet on the fire, especially if there be meat [cooking] before it. In polite society, do not turn your back to the fire and do not approach it closer than others—for these are the privileges of persons of rank. When there is a need for stirring the fire, putting wood on or pulling or lifting it, this is the job of the person who has the general superintendence of those things.

When seated, place your feet firmly on the ground, with the legs at an equal distance, and neither a leg nor a foot should be crossed one upon the other.

When in public, it is insufferable breach of etiquette to stretch out one's body by extending the arms, or to assume different postures. It is absolutely forbidden to pare your nails in public; and also, do not gnaw your nails.

Do not shake the head, nor fidget the legs, nor roll the eyes, nor frown, nor twist the mouth. Take care not to let saliva escape with your words, and do not let spittle fly into the faces of those with whom you converse. To prevent such an accident, do not approach your conversant too near; but engage in conversation at a reasonable distance.

Do not stop to kill lice or any other disgusting animals of this kind in the presence of your company. If anything on the ground, such as phlegm or spittle, offends the sight, then put your foot on it. If it is on the garment of someone with whom you are conversing, do not show it to him or to anyone else, but do your best to remove it unobserved. If someone obliges you in this way, make your acknowledgments to him.

Turn not your back to others, especially in speaking. Jog not the table or desk on which another reads or writes. Do not lean against anyone, or pull at anyone's clothes while you entertain them in conversation.

Do not stop in conversation to adjust garters or pull up stockings to appear more gallant. Do not allow your nails to be dirty or too long. Take great care for the cleanliness of your hands, but do not overdo it.

It is a very low act to puff up the cheeks, to stick out the tongue, to pull on one's beard, to rub one's hands, to chew or bite on the lips, or to hold the mouth too widely open or too tightly closed.

Do not flatter or wheedle anyone with fine words, for he who aspires to gain another's favor by his honeyed words shows that the speaker does not regard him in high esteem, and that the speaker deems him far from sensible or clever, in taking him for a man who may be tricked in this manner.

Do not play practical jokes on those who would take as an offense.

It is an act directly opposed to good manners to read a book, letters or similar things during ordinary conversation if it is not a pressing matter, or resolved very quickly; and even in that case, it is proper to ask permission unless you are, possibly, the highest in rank of the company. It is even worse to handle other people's work, their books or things of that nature, to get too near to these objects, to look at them closely without the owner's permission, and also to praise or find fault with them before your opinion has been asked; or to approach too close and inconvenience anyone when he is reading his letters or other papers.

The face should not look fantastic, changeable, absent, rapt in attention, covered with sadness, various or volatile; and it should not show any signs of an unquiet mind. On the contrary, it should be open and tranquil, but not too expansive with joy in serious affairs, nor too self-contained by an affected gravity in the ordinary and familiar conversation of human life.

The gestures of the body must be suited to the discourse you are upon.

Reproach none for their infirmities. Avoid it equally when they are natural ones, and do not take pleasure in uttering words that cause anyone shame, whoever it may be.

Show not yourself glad at the misfortune of an other, though he were your enemy. It argues a mischievous mind, that you had a desire to have done it yourself, and if you had the power or opportunity to, you would have.

When you see a crime punished, you may be inwardly pleased; but always show pity to the suffering offender.

Do not laugh too loud or too much at any public spectacle lest you cause yourself to be laughed at.

Superfluous compliments and all affectation of ceremony are to be avoided; yet where due, they are not to be neglected.

In pulling off your hat to persons of distinction, make a reverence, bowing more or less according to the custom of the better bred and quality of persons. Amongst equals, expect not always that they should begin with you first; but to pull off the hat when there is no need is affectation. In the manner of salutation, keep to the most usual custom.

It is ill manners to bid one more eminent than yourself to put on his hat, as well as not to do so when it is due. Likewise, he that makes too much haste to put on his hat does not well, yet he ought to put it on at the first, or at most the second time of being asked. All of these remarks on polite conduct must also be extended to the order to be observed in taking places and in sitting down. Ceremonies without bounds are troublesome.

If anyone comes to speak to you while you are sitting, stand up although he be your inferior. And when you present seats, let it be to everyone according to his rank.

When you meet with one of greater quality than yourself, stop and retire, especially if it be at a door or any straight place, to give way for him to pass.

In walking, the highest place in most countries seems to be on the right hand. Therefore, place yourself on the left of him whom you desire to honor. If three walk together, the middle place is the most honorable. The wall is usually given to the most worthy if two walk together.

If anyone far surpasses others, either in age, estate, or merit, yet in any particular instance would give place to one less than himself (in his own house or elsewhere) the lesser one ought not to accept it. Also, the superior, for fear of making himself uncivil, ought not to press it above once or twice.

To one who is your equal, or not much inferior, you give the chief place in your lodging. And he to whom it is offered ought, at the first to refuse, but at the second offer to accept, though not without acknowledging his own unworthiness.

They that are in dignity or in office have, in all places, precedency. But while they are young, they ought to respect those that are their equals in birth or other qualities, even though they have no public charge.

It is the height of politeness always to speak better of those with whom we converse than of ourselves. Particularly when they are persons of a superior rank to ourselves, with whom we ought never to dispute in any fashion.

Let your discourse with men of business be short and comprehensive. One should spare them and make himself understood rather by looks than by words.

Craftsman and persons of low degree ought not to use many ceremonies to disturb their superiors or others of high rank, but respect and honor them. Those of high rank ought to treat their lessers with affability and courtesy, without arrogancy.

In speaking to men of quality, do not lean, nor look them full in the face, nor approach too near them. At the least, keep a full step in distance.

In visiting the sick, do not act the physician if you are not trained in that science.

In writing or speaking, give to every person his due title, according to his degree and the custom of the place.

Strive not with your superiors in argument, but always submit your judgment to others with modesty.

Undertake not to teach your equal in the art that he himself professes. It flavours of arrogancy.

Let your ceremonies in courtesy be proper to the dignity of the place of the person with whom you converse. It is absurd to act the same with a clown and a Prince.

Do not express joy before one who is sick or in pain, for that contrary passion will aggravate his misery.

When a man does all he can, though it succeeds not well, blame not he that did it since he is more worthy of praise than blame.

To advise or reprehend anyone, consider whether it ought to be public or in private, presently or at some other time, in what terms to do it and, in reproving, show no signs of choler, but do it with all sweetness and mildness.

Take all admonitions thankfully, in what time or place whatsoever given, but afterwards, not being culpable, take a time or place convenient to let him know it that gave them.

Mock not, nor jest at anything of importance. Make no jests that are sharp and biting, and if you deliver anything witty and pleasant, abstain from laughing thereat yourself.

Wherein you reprove another, be unblameful yourself. Example is more prevalent than precept.

Use no reproachful language against anyone. Neither curse nor revile.

Do not be hasty to believe flying reports to the disparagement of any one.

Wear not your clothes foul, ripped or dusty, but see to it that they be brushed once every day at least. Take heed that you approach not to any uncleanness.

In your apparel, be modest and endeavor to accommodate nature rather than procure admiration. Keep to the fashion of your equals, such as are civil and orderly, with respect to times and places.

Run not in the streets. Neither go too slowly nor with mouth open. Go not shaking your arms, stamping or shuffling, nor pull up your stockings in the street. Walk not upon your toes, nor in a dancing or skipping manner, nor yet with measured steps. Strike not the heels together, nor stoop when there is no occasion.

Play not the peacock, looking everywhere about you to see if you be well decked, if your shoes fit well, if your stockings sit neatly, and your clothes appear handsomely.

Eat not in the streets, nor in your house out of the normal meal times; at least abstain from it in the presence of others.

Associate yourself with men of good quality if you esteem your own reputation. For 'tis better to be alone than in bad company.

In walking about the house alone with a person whose rank demands some deference, at the first step be sure to give him your right hand. Stop not walking until he does. Do not be the first to turn. If you do turn, let it be with your face towards him. If he be a man of great quality, walk not with him cheek by jowl but somewhat behind him, but yet in such a manner that he may easily speak to you.

Let your conversation be without malice or envy, for 'tis a sign of a tractable and commendable nature. And in all causes of passion admit reason to govern.

Never express anything unbecoming, nor act against moral Rules, especially in front of your inferiors.

Be not immodest in urging your friends to discover their secrets.

Utter not base or frivolous things amongst grave and learned men; nor very difficult questions or subjects, nor things hard to be believed, among the ignorant. Stuff not your discourse with proverbs when you are amongst your betters or your equals.

Speak not of sad things in a time of mirth, or at the table. Speak not of melancholy things such as death and wounds, and if others mention them, change the discourse if you can. Tell not your dreams but to your intimate friends.

"Washington, always beloved as a citizen, an officer and a gentleman,
is America's mystical icon of heroic grace."

2 "...Martha Washington was the ideal woman for the new American republic. She was not born of the aristocracy, but she gained the admiration and respect of all classes of people."

3 "In 1745, sixteen-year-old George came to live at Mount Vernon. This serendipity gave young George a life of culture and connections."

A man ought not to value himself of his achievements or rare qualities, his riches, his titles, his virtue or his kindred. But he need not speak meanly of himself either.

Jesting must be avoided when it is inappropriate. Laugh not aloud, nor at all without occasion. Deride no man's misfortune, although there may seem to be some cause.

Speak not injurious words, neither in jest nor earnest. Scoff at no one, although they give occasion.

Be not rude, but friendly and courteous. Be the first to salute, to hear, to answer; and be not pensive when it is time to converse.

Detract not from others; neither be excessive in commending them.

Go not thither where you know not whether you shall be welcome or not. Give not advice without being asked and, when desired, do it briefly.

If two contend together, take not the part of either unless some greater reason obliges you to do so. And be not obstinate in your opinion. In things to which you are indifferent, be a part of the majority.

Reprehend not the imperfections of others for that is the province of parents, masters, superiors.

Gaze not at the marks or blemishes of others, and ask not how they came. What you may speak in secret to your friend, deliver not before others.

Speak not in an unknown tongue in company, but in your own language as those of quality do, and not as the vulgar world would. Sublime matters treat seriously.

Think before you speak. Pronounce not imperfectly nor bring out your words too hastily, but orderly and distinctly.

When another speaks, be attentive yourself and disturb not the audience. If any hesitate in his words, help him not, nor prompt him without it being desired; interrupt him not, nor answer him until his speech be ended.

In the midst of discourse, ask not what it is about. But if you perceive any stop because of your arrival, rather, request the speaker to continue. If a person of quality comes in while you converse, it is gracious to repeat what was said before.

While you are talking, point not with your finger at him whom you discourse, nor approach too near to whom you talk, especially to his face.

Treat with men at fit times about business, and whisper not in the company of others.

Make no comparisons, and if any of the company be commended for any brave act or virtue, commend not another for the same.

Be not apt to relate news if you know not the truth thereof. In discoursing of things that you have heard, name not your author. Do not reveal a secret.

Be not tedious in discourse or in reading, unless you find the company to be pleased therewith.

Be not curious to know the affairs of others. Do not approach near to those who speak in private.

Undertake not what you cannot perform. Be careful to keep your promises.

When you fulfill a mission, do it without passion and with discretion, however mean the person be for whom you do it.

When your superiors talk, listen eagerly and neither speak nor laugh.

In the company of those of higher quality than yourself, speak not until you are asked a question. Then stand upright, put off your hat, and answer in a few words.

In disputes, be not so desirous to overcome objections as not to give liberty to each one to deliver his opinion, and submit to the judgment of the majority, especially if they are judges of the dispute.

Let your bearing be such as becomes a man who is grave, settled and attentive to what is said, without being too serious. Contradict not at every turn what others say.

Be not tedious in discourse; make not many digressions; nor repeat often the same manner of discourse.

Speak not evil of those who are absent, for it is unjust.

When dining, scratch not, neither spit, cough nor blow your nose, except when there is a necessity for it.

Make no show of taking great delight in your food. Feed not with greediness. Cut your bread with a knife. Lean not on the table. Do not find fault with what you have to eat.

Take no salt, nor cut bread when your knife is greasy.

When entertaining someone, it is polite to serve him at table and present the dishes of food to him. When invited by another, it is more polite to wait to be served by the host, or someone else unless invited by the host to help himself to the food. Avoid being officious in helping others when not in one's own house, where one has little authority unless the host cannot attend to everything. In that case, help the ones nearest.

If you soak bread in the sauce, let it be no more than what you put in your mouth at one time. Blow not on your broth at the table, but wait until it cools of itself.

Put not your meat to your mouth with your knife in your hand. Neither spit forth the stones of any fruit pie upon a dish, nor cast anything under the table.

It is not polite to stoop too close into one's meat. Keep fingers clean, and when foul, wipe them on a corner of your table napkin.

Put not another bite into your mouth until the former be swallowed. Let not your morsels be too big for your jowls.

Drink not, nor talk with your mouth full. Neither gaze about while you are drinking.

Drink not too leisurely, nor yet too hastily. Wipe your lips before and after drinking. Breathe not when drinking, or ever with too great a noise for it is uncivil.

Cleanse not your teeth with the tablecloth, napkin, fork or knife; but if others do it, let it be done with a tooth pick.

Rinse not your mouth in the presence of others.

It is out of fashion to call upon others often to eat. Nor need you drink to others every time you eat.

In the company of your betters, be not longer in eating than they are. Lay not your arm, but arise with only a touch on the end of the table.

The most distinguished member of the company is first to unfold his napkin and touch the food. The rest should graciously wait without touching the food before he does.

Be not angry at table, whatsoever happens, and if you have reason to be so, show it not. Put on a cheerful countenance, especially if there be strangers, for good humor makes one dish of meat a feast.

Do not place yourself at the head of the table unless it be your due or the master of the house would have it so. Contend not lest you should trouble the company.

If others talk at table, be attentive. But talk not with meat in your mouth.

When you speak of God or His attributes, be serious and speak with words of reverence. Honor and obey your natural parents, although they may be poor.

Let your recreations be manful, and not sinful.

Labor to keep alive in your breast that little spark of celestial fire called conscience.

* * *

George Washington was a wise friend to more diverse Americans than any other man of his times.

"He knew officers, generals and privates; Frenchmen and Englishmen; Yankees and Southern planters; frontiersmen and Quakers. He dealt with Indians who were enemies and Indians who were allies; with blacks who were slaves, who were freemen, and who were his own soldiers. His ability to deal with all of them was founded on his training in these rules [110 Rules for Young Gentlemen, also known as *The Rules of Civility*]."

CHAPTER THREE

Washington's Prayers

*That an All Powerful Providence may keep us both
in safety is the prayer of your ever faithful and
affectionate Friend.*[54]
—George Washington

merica's civility is deeply rooted in spirituality. The
Founders, diversely spiritual, wanted God in public
life, but knew all too well the religious warfare that could
destroy whole governments. Benjamin Franklin and Thomas
Jefferson had personal experience in France as U.S. diplomats during the era leading up to and commencing the
French Revolution. These two men were adamant in com-
municating to Washington their belief that the preservation
of human freedom rests on the ability of reasonable people
to be adequately informed. Their experiences abroad provided invaluable insights for American leaders who wanted
no part of the anarchistic French reign of terror in the
American example of republican government. Jefferson, in
fact, wrote the statute of Virginia for religious freedom. He

founded the University of Virginia; Franklin founded the University of Pennsylvania.

The Founders, with George Washington their leader, were exquisitely careful to distinguish between private and public religion. In private, Americans were inspired by the Founders to practice their religious beliefs to the utmost of their abilities. In the public business of government however, they were careful to speak of God "in a way that was unifying, not divisive. 'Nature's God' was the path they chose."[55]

A small manuscript book entitled "Daily Sacrifice," said to be in the handwriting of twenty-year-old George Washington, disclosing a personal and intimate visage of Washington's purported private, Christian prayer life, was sold at auction as such by Washington's heirs in Philadelphia on April 21, 1891. Washington's family said he prayed these prayers daily each day of the week.[56] The most hallowed of all his writings, these remnants of what is believed to be Washington's personal prayer book are written on twenty-four pages of a small journal about the size of an ordinary pocket memorandum. No one knows whether these prayers were originals, or if Washington copied them from another source.[57]

Reverend Dr. Tim LeHaye, co-author of the bestselling *Left Behind* series says, these prayers of George Washington reveal "many of his [George Washington] theological beliefs about God, Jesus Christ, sin, salvation, eternal life, and himself as a humble servant of Jesus Christ."[58] Realizing he was expected to remain faithful to God's Plan for him throughout all of life's stages and challenges, George Washington called to God, relied on God, trusted in God's kindness as his record and writings disclose, bent to God's ways as revealed in Scripture, blessed God in good times and in adversity. Washington's daily prayers enriched his faith as he sought holiness and happiness. Such faith is a gift from God and like all living things; it must be nurtured if it is to grow.

Washington feared God, yet trusted that God is "Father of All Mercies" and he addressed The Deity as such.[59] Spiritually astute Washington was aware that no one knows Jesus Christ the Savior unless the Eternal Father reveals His Son.[60] Washington understood that God's mercy is His reward for those who sincerely seek Him. He recognized every man as a redeemed child of God's love whether he knew Jesus by name or not. He believed that fear of the Lord is the beginning of knowledge; Washington dared not interfere in God's timetable of revelation for others.[61]

George Washington wisely respected every man's authentic faith tradition, although God's only begotten Son, Jesus Christ, was the Light of his life. He informed his troops: "The General [Washington] hopes and trusts, that every officer and man, will endeavor so to live, and act, as becomes a Christian Soldier defending the dearest Rights and Liberties of his country."[62]

Washington cherished his Christian heritage enough to live it to the fullest. Though his public life was carefully steeped in the politically correct diplomatic language of the Enlightenment, Washington never wavered in his private, personal, Christian commitments. Occasionally, he shared segments of his own deeply private concept of God's mercy. In a speech to the Delaware Chiefs in 1789, Washington said: "You do well to wish to learn our arts and ways of life and above all the religion of Jesus Christ."

Washington was a lifelong, practicing member of an ancient Christian denomination; Anglicanism (Episcopalian in the United States after the Revolution) traces its origins to Roman Catholicism. He publicly recited the Nicene Creed (see Appendix II) during church services, which he attended regularly.[63] His family, troops, cabinet and colleagues attested that he continuously sought God's grace to help his human acts achieve goodness, justice and triumph over every sort of defeat. Each American is a beneficiary of George Washington's prayers. They contain seeds of strength and renewal sufficient to have sustained and ennobled the "Foundingist of the Founders".[64]

Of course, there have always been, and probably always will be doubters who question the veracity of things as personal and life-giving as George Washington's prayer life. The handwritten prayers attributed to him are so humbly and thoroughly Christian that it follows as night the day they will encounter controversy. They have survived more than two hundred years. His family spoke of Washington's handwritten prayers and the general's devout use of them. Through the years untold numbers have also found inspiration and solace in these simple and heartfelt prayers. They reveal a humble and contrite heart which God does not spurn.

Washington's prayers, whatever they were, and however he said them drew down God's mercy, "a kind Providence" upon the American people. "George Washington's Prayers", slightly edited to conform to modern usage, continue to sustain and ennoble people who sincerely pray them.

* * *

George Washington's Sunday Morning Prayer

Almighty God, and most merciful Father,
who commanded the children of Israel to offer a daily
sacrifice to Thee,
that thereby they might glorify and praise Thee
for Thy protection both night and day;
receive, O Lord, my morning sacrifice which I now offer
up to Thee;
I yield Thee humble and hearty thanks
that Thou hast preserved me from the dangers of the
night past,
and brought me to the light of this day,
and the comforts thereof,
a day which is consecrated to Thine own service
and for Thine own honor.
Let my heart therefore, Gracious God,
be so affected with the glory and majesty of it,
that I may not do mine own works, but wait on Thee,
and discharge those weighty duties Thou require of me;
and since Thou art a God of pure eyes,
and will be sanctified in all who draw near unto Thee,
who doest not regard the sacrifice of fools,
nor hear sinners who tread in Thy courts,
pardon, I beseech Thee, my sins,
remove them from Thy presence,
as far as the east is from the west,
and accept of me for the merits of Thy son Jesus Christ,
that when I come into Thy temple,

and compass Thy altar,

my prayers may come before Thee as incense;

and as Thou wouldst hear me calling upon Thee in my prayers, so give me grace to hear Thee calling on me in Thy word, that it may be wisdom, righteousness, reconciliation

and peace to the saving of my soul in the day of the Lord Jesus.

Grant that I may hear it with reverence,

receive it with meekness, mingle it with faith,

and that it may accomplish in me, Gracious God,

the good work for which Thou hast sent it.

Bless my family, kindred, friends, and country,

be our God & guide this day and forever for His sake,

who lay down in the Grave and arose again for us,

Jesus Christ our Lord. Amen.

* * *

George Washington's Sunday Evening Prayer

O most glorious God, in Jesus Christ my merciful and loving father,

I acknowledge and confess my guilt,

in the weak and imperfect performance of the duties of this day.

I have called on Thee for pardon and forgiveness of sins, but so coldly and carelessly, that my prayers are become my sin

and stand in need of pardon.

I have heard Thy Holy Word, but with such deadness of spirit that I have been an unprofitable and forgetful hearer,

so that O Lord, tho' I have done Thy work

yet it hath been so negligently

that I may rather expect a curse than a blessing from Thee. But, O God, who art rich in mercy and plenteous in redemption,

mark not, I beseech Thee, what I have done amiss;

remember that I am but dust,

and remit my transgressions, negligence & ignorance,

and cover them all with the absolute obedience of Thy dear Son,

that those sacrifices which I have offered

may be accepted by Thee, in and for the sacrifice

of Jesus Christ offered upon the cross for me;

for His sake, ease me of the burdens of my sins,

and give me grace that by the call of the Gospel

I may rise from the slumber of sin into the newness of life. Let me live according to those holy rules which

Thou hast this day prescribed in Thy holy word.

Make me to know what is acceptable in Thy sight,

and therein to delight.

Open the eyes of my understanding,

and help me thoroughly to examine myself

concerning my knowledge, faith and repentance.

Increase my faith, and direct me to the true object,

Jesus Christ, the way, the truth and the life.

Bless O Lord all the people of this land,

from the highest to the lowest, particularly those whom

Thou hast appointed to rule over us in church and state. Continue Thy goodness to me this night.

These weak petitions I humbly implore Thee to hear,

accept and answer for the sake of Thy dear Son
Jesus Christ, our Lord. Amen.

* * *

George Washington's Monday Morning Prayer

O Eternal and everlasting God,

I presume to present myself this morning before Thy
Divine majesty

and beseech Thee to accept of my humble and hearty
thanks, that it has pleased Thy great goodness to keep and
preserve me this night from all the dangers poor mortals are
subject to.

Thou has given me sweet and pleasant sleep, whereby I
find my body refreshed and comforted for performing the
duties of this day,

in which I beseech Thee to defend me from all perils of
body and soul.

Direct my thoughts, words and work.

Wash away my sins in the immaculate blood of the lamb.

Purge my heart by Thy Holy Spirit, from the dross of my
natural corruption,

that I may with more freedom of mind and liberty of will
serve Thee, the ever lasting God,

in righteous and holiness this day, and all the days of my
life.

Increase my faith in the sweet promises of the Gospel;

give me repentance from dead works;

pardon my wanderings and direct my thoughts unto
Thyself, the God of my salvation.

Teach me how to live in Thy fear, labor in Thy service, and ever to run in the ways on Thy commandments.

Make me always watchful over my heart,

that neither the terrors of conscience, the loathing of holy duties, the love of sin, nor an unwillingness to depart this life, may cast me into a spiritual slumber.

But daily frame me more and more into the likeness of Thy Son, Jesus Christ,

that living in Thy fear, and dying in Thy favor,

I may in Thy appointed time attain the resurrection of the just unto eternal life.

Bless my family, friends and kindred.

Unite us all in praising and glorifying Thee in all our works begun, continued, and ended when we shall come to make our last account before Thee, Blessed Savior, who has taught us thus to pray.

Our Father, who art in Heaven, hallowed be Thy Name.

Thy Kingdom come.

Thy will be done on earth as it is in Heaven.

Give us this day our daily bread.

Forgive us our trespasses as we forgive those who trespass against us.

Lead us not into temptation but deliver us from evil.

For Thine is the Kingdom, the power and the glory forever. Amen.

* * *

George Washington's Monday Evening Prayer

Most gracious Lord God, from whom proceeds every good and perfect gift,

I offer to Thy Divine Majesty my unfeigned praise and thanksgiving for all Thy mercies toward me.

Thou made me at first and hast ever since sustained the work of Thine own hand.

Thou gave Thy Son to die for me,

and has given me assurance of salvation upon my repentance and sincerely endeavoring to conform my life to His holy precepts and example.

Thou art pleased to lengthen out to me the time of repentance

and to move me to it by Thy Spirit and by Thy Word, by Thy mercies and by Thy judgments.

Out of a deepness of Thy mercies, and my own unworthiness

I do appear before Thee at this time.

I have sinned and done very wickedly,

be merciful to me O, God, and pardon me for Jesus Christ's sake.

Instruct me in the particulars of my duty.

Suffer me not to be tempted above what Thou have given me strength to bear.

Take care, I pray Thee, of my affairs and more and more direct me in Thy truth.

Defend me from my enemies, especially my spiritual ones. Suffer me not to be drawn from Thee, by the blandishments of the world, carnal desires, the cunning of the devil, or deceitfulness of sin.

Work in me Thy good will and pleasure,

and discharge my mind from all things that are displeasing to Thee,

of all ill will and discontent, wrath and bitterness, pride and vain conceit of myself

and render me charitable, pure, holy, patient and heavenly minded.

Be with me at the hour of death; dispose me for it,

and deliver me from the slavish fear of it.

Make me willing and fit to die whenever Thou shall call me hence.

Bless our rulers in Church and State.

Bless O Lord the whole race of mankind,

and let the world be filled with the knowledge of Thee and Thy Son, Jesus Christ.

Pity the sick, the poor, the weak, the needy, the widows and fatherless,

and all that mourn or are broken in heart,

and be merciful to them according to their several necessities.

Bless my friends and give me grace to forgive my enemies as heartily as I desire forgiveness of Thee my Heavenly Father.

I beseech Thee to defend me this night from all evil,

and do more for me than I can think to ask,

for Jesus Christ's sake, in whose most holy name and words, I continue to pray.

Our Father, who art in Heaven, hallowed be Thy Name.

Thy Kingdom come.

Thy will be done on earth as it is in Heaven.

Give us this day our daily bread.

Forgive us our trespasses as we forgive those who trespass against us.

Lead us not into temptation but deliver us from evil.

For Thine is the Kingdom, the power and the glory forever. Amen.

* * *

George Washington's Tuesday Morning Prayer

O Lord our God, most mighty and merciful Father,

I Thine unworthy creature and servant do once more approach Thy presence.

Though not worthy to appear before Thee because of my natural corruptions,

and the many sins and transgressions which I have committed against Thy divine majesty,

yet I beseech Thee, for the sake of Him in whom Thou are well pleased, the Lord Jesus Christ,

to admit me to render Thee deserved thanks and praises for Thy manifold mercies extended toward me,

for the quiet rest and repose of the past night,

for food, raiment, health, peace, liberty, and the hopes of a better life through the merits of Thy dear Son's bitter passion.

O kind Father, continue Thy mercy and favor to me this day and ever hereafter.

Prosper all my lawful undertakings.

Let me have all my directions from Thy Holy Spirit, and success from Thy bountiful hand.

Let the bright beams of Thy light so shine into my heart, and enlighten my mind in understanding Thy blessed word, that I may be enabled to perform Thy will in all things,

and effectually resist all temptations of the world, the flesh and the devil.

Preserve and defend our rulers in Church and State.

Bless the people of this land.

Be a father to the fatherless,

a comforter to the comfortless,

a deliverer to the captives and a physician to the sick.

Let Thy blessings be upon our friends, kindred and families. Be our guide this day and forever through Jesus Christ,

in whose blessed form of prayer I conclude my weak petitions.

Our Father, who art in Heaven, hallowed be Thy Name.

Thy Kingdom come.

Thy will be done on earth as it is in Heaven.

Give us this day our daily bread.

Forgive us our trespasses as we forgive those who trespass against us.

Lead us not into temptation but deliver us from evil.

For Thine is the Kingdom, the power and the glory forever. Amen.

* * *

George Washington's Tuesday Evening Prayer

Most gracious God and Heavenly Father,
we cannot cease, but must cry unto Thee for mercy,
because my sins cry against me for justice.
How shall I address myself unto Thee.
I must with the publican stand and admire at Thy great goodness, tender mercy, and long suffering toward me,
in that Thou has kept me the past day from being consumed and brought to naught.
O Lord, what is man, or the son of man, that Thou regard him.
The more days pass over my head the more sins and iniquities I heap up against Thee.
If I should cast up the account of my good deeds done this day, how few and small they would be.
But if I should reckon my transgressions, surely they would be many and great.
O blessed Father,
let Thy Son's blood wash me from all impurities,
and cleanse me from the stains of sin that are upon me.
Give me grace to lay hold upon His merits,
that they may be my reconciliation and atonement unto Thee—that I may know my sins are forgiven by His passion and death.
Embrace me in the arms of Thy mercy.
Vouchsafe to receive me unto the bosom of Thy love.
Shadow me with Thy wings,
that I may safely rest under Thy protection this night.

And so unto Thy hands I commend myself, both soul and body, in the name of Thy Son, Jesus Christ,

beseeching Thee, when this life shall end,

I may take my everlasting rest with Thee in Thy heavenly Kingdom.

Bless all in authority over us.

Be merciful with all those afflicted with Thy cross or calamity.

Bless all my friends, forgive all my enemies,

and accept my thanksgiving this evening for the mercies and favors afforded me.

Hear and graciously answer these, my requests,

and whatever else Thou see needful grant us,

for the sake of Jesus Christ in whose blessed name and words I continue to pray.

Our Father, who art in Heaven, hallowed be Thy Name.

Thy Kingdom come.

Thy will be done on earth as it is in Heaven.

Give us this day our daily bread.

Forgive us our trespasses as we forgive those who trespass against us.

Lead us not into temptation but deliver us from evil.

For Thine is the Kingdom, the power and the glory forever. Amen.

* * *

George Washington's Wednesday Morning Prayer

Almighty and eternal Lord God,

the great Creator of Heaven and earth,

and the God and Father of our Lord Jesus Christ,

look down from Heaven, in pity and compassion upon me Thy servant,

who humbly prostrate myself before Thee,

sensible of Thy mercy and my own misery.

There is an infinite distance between Thy glorious majesty and me, Thy poor creature, the work of Thy hand,

between Thy infinite power, and my weakness,

Thy wisdom and my folly,

Thy eternal Being, and my mortal frame.

But O Lord, I have set myself at a greater distance from Thee by my sin and wickedness,

and humbly acknowledge the corruption of my nature and the many rebellions of my life.

I have sinned against heaven and before Thee,

in thought, word and deed.

I have contemned Thy majesty and holy laws.

I have likewise sinned by omitting what I ought to have done, and committing what I ought not.

I have rebelled against light, despised Thy mercies and judgments, and broken my vows and promises.

I have neglected the means of Grace and opportunities of becoming better.

My iniquities are multiplied and my sins are very great.

I confess them, o Lord, with shame and sorrow, detestation and loathing,

and desire to be vile in my own eyes, as I have rendered myself vile in Thine.

I humbly beseech Thee to be merciful to me in the free pardon of my sins, for the sake of Thy dear Son, my only Savior, Jesus Christ, who came not to call the righteous, but sinners to repentance.

Be pleased to renew my nature and write Thy laws upon my heart.

Help me to live righteously, soberly, and godly in this evil world.

Make me humble, meek, patient, and contented,

and work in me the grace of Thy Holy Spirit.

Prepare me for death and judgment,

and let the thoughts thereof awaken me to greater care and study to approve myself unto Thee in well doing.

Bless our rulers in church and State.

Help all in affliction or adversity—give them patience and a sanctified use of their affliction,

and in Thy good time, deliverance from them.

Forgive my enemies; take me unto Thy protection this day. Keep me in perfect peace, which I ask in the name and for the sake of Jesus in whose name I pray.

Our Father, who art in Heaven, hallowed be Thy Name.

Thy Kingdom come.

Thy will be done on earth as it is in Heaven.

Give us this day our daily bread.

Forgive us our trespasses as we forgive those who trespass against us.

Lead us not into temptation but deliver us from evil.

For Thine is the Kingdom, the power and the glory forever. Amen.

* * *

George Washington's Wednesday Evening Prayer

Holy and eternal Lord God who art the King of Heaven,
and the watchman of Israel,
that never slumber or sleep,
what shall we render unto Thee for all Thy benefits.
Because Thou hast inclined Thine ears unto me,
therefore will I call on Thee as long as I live.
From the rising of the sun to the going down of the
same, let Thy name be praised.
Among the infinite riches of Thy mercy towards me,
I desire to render thanks and praise for Thy merciful
preservation of me this day,
as well as all the days of my life,
and for Thy many other blessings and mercies, spiritual
and temporal which Thou hast bestowed upon me,
contrary to my deserving.
All these Thy mercies call on me to be thankful
and my infirmities and wants call for a continuance of
Thy tender mercies.
Cleanse my soul O Lord, I beseech Thee,
from whatever is offensive to Thee, and hurtful to me,
and give me what is convenient for me.
Watch over me this night,
and give me comfortable and sweet sleep to fit me for the
service of the day following.
Let my soul watch for the coming of the Lord Jesus.
Let my bed put me in mind of my grave,
and my rising from there of my last Resurrection.
O Heavenly Father, so frame this heart of mine,

that I may ever delight to live according to Thy will and command,

in holiness and righteousness before Thee all the days of my life.

Let me remember O Lord,

the time will come when the trumpet shall sound,

and the dead shall arise and stand before the judgment seat, and give an account of whatever they have done in the body. Let me so prepare my soul that I may do it with joy

and not with grief

Bless the rulers and people of this land

and forget not those who are under any affliction or oppression.

Let Thy favor be extended to all my relations, friends, and all others I ought to remember in my prayers.

Hear me I beseech Thee

for the sake of my dear Redeemer in whose holy words, I farther pray.

Our Father, who art in Heaven, hallowed be Thy Name.

Thy Kingdom come.

Thy will be done on earth as it is in Heaven.

Give us this day our daily bread.

Forgive us our trespasses as we forgive those who trespass against us.

Lead us not into temptation but deliver us from evil.

For Thine is the Kingdom, the power and the glory forever. Amen.

* * *

George Washington's Thursday Morning Prayer

Most gracious Lord God, whose dwelling is in the highest heavens,
    and yet behold the lowly and humble upon earth,
I blush and am ashamed to lift up my eyes to Thy dwelling place,
    because I have sinned against Thee.
Look down I beseech Thee upon me, Thine unworthy servant
    who prostrate myself at the footstool of Thy mercy, confessing my own guiltiness,
    and begging pardon for my sins.
What couldst Thou have done Lord more for me,
or what could I have done more against Thee?
Thou didst send me Thy Son to take our nature upon—

* * *

The manuscript ended here at the close of that page. For some, the question of the authenticity of the handwritten pages remains an open one. Final settlement may depend upon some sort of definitive demonstration that they are unquestionably from the hand of George Washington.[65] The handwritten prayers can be viewed on the Internet at http://personal.pitnet.net/primarysources/george.html, among other sites.

PART TWO

Freedom's Cost

Listen! The Great Spirit protects that man [George Washington], and guides his destinies—he will become the chief of nations, and a people yet unborn will hail him as the founder of a mighty empire …[66]

Prophesy of an aged Indian chief in the
Ohio Valley, circa 1772

CHAPTER FOUR

Washington's Early Military Experience

"Good moral character is the first essential in a man."[67]
—George Washington

George Washington looked to his elder half-brother Lawrence for guidance and economic assistance during his adolescence. In 1743, Lawrence married Anne Fairfax, daughter of Virginia land magnate Colonel William Fairfax, proprietor of millions of acres of colonial property. He brought his bride to live at the estate he inherited from his father at Little Hunting Creek on the Potomac River. Lawrence named his home Mount Vernon, in honor of his Commanding Officer, Admiral Edward Vernon, under whom he had served as an officer in 1741, during the British siege of the Spanish Caribbean port of Cartagena.

In 1745, sixteen-year-old George came to live at Mount Vernon. This serendipity gave young George a life of culture and connections. "…George was welcomed not only at Mount Vernon but at Belvoir [the Fairfax estate], as well. Indeed, Belvoir became something of a finishing school for George in his impressionable teenage years, and he learned first hand how the elite in Virginia society conducted themselves. With its handsome and commodious rooms adorned by luxurious carpets and rich furniture imported from England, Belvoir was one of the finest homes in the colony."[68]

At age 16 George was:

"…physically his father's son, and in strength, almost a man. He was systematic, he had achieved his ambition of learning to write swiftly and clearly, and he could perform readily enough the simple mathematical problems of surveying. His mind found interest chiefly in matters of business, concerning which he was mature beyond his age, though he had little imagination except for planning how he could advance himself…He rode admirably. He made on adults an excellent impression of vitality, courtesy and integrity at the same time that he won the good will of the young. Along with these excellencies, he had the softness of the young gentleman who would ride horseback by the hour but always would come back to a comfortable house and a good bed. Although he was far from rich, he was accustomed to an ease quite different from the life of the frontier. Instead of wearing a hunting shirt and telling time 'by the sun' he carried a watch and enjoyed some of the clothes of fashion."[69]

George Washington's life of ease would be short-lived, though his refined taste would help build a new nation out of the harsh wilderness. Washington was learning how to bring order out of chaos.

His first job at seventeen was as the youngest surveyor ever appointed in Virginia; he became the official surveyor for the County of Culpepper. In this position, George learned how to survive on the frontier. He also became adept at recognizing the value of fine real estate. By the time he was 20 years old, and earning about 100 pounds a year, George purchased 2,000 acres of land in the Shenandoah Valley.

Upon Lawrence's untimely death from tuberculosis in 1752, twenty-two-year-old George was appointed to his half-brother's position as military adjutant for the Southern District of Virginia, and subsequently for the Northern Neck and Eastern Shore.[70] George rented Mount Vernon from his deceased brother's widow. Lawrence had provided in his will that his property at Mount Vernon would pass to his wife and then to their living children. If none would survive, Lawrence devised to his young brother George a reversionary interest in Mount Vernon.[71] Consequently, after the death of his sister-in-law, all of whose four children had predeceased her, George Washington acquired a life interest in Mount Vernon for himself and his spouse.

Because of his limited financial means, George did not attend college, though his father and elder half-brothers had been educated in England.[72] Washington's mother may not have approved of the value of higher education because of her own limited means, and she may have expected her first born son to be a provider.

Driven, motivated, and self-taught, Washington developed his character through his love of manly sports and long hours in the vast wilderness on horseback as a surveyor and military leader. No stranger to letters, Washington enjoyed the erudition of Stoic philosophy, especially Plutarch's *Lives*, Addison's *Cato* and Seneca's *Dialogues*.[73] These works, coupled with his prayer life rooted in the Bible, filled his mind and soul with dreams and goals.

Washington's bold horsemanship, modesty and expertise at fox hunting endeared him to the Fairfax family. He continued to pass many happy hours at Belvoir enjoying the expertise and business acumen of Lord Fairfax. George suspected that great profits awaited settlers beyond the Allegheny Mountains and Lord Fairfax encouraged Washington to seek his fortune in the western wilderness.

During his early western travels, Washington found vast tracts of rich, fertile land, magnificent fruit-filled trees, and rivers and streams sparkling with fish. He observed Indian customs, and their weakness for hard liquor. As a young Major in the Virginia Militia, Washington had many encounters with wary tribal chiefs. He appreciated and respected the native tribes' attachment to these bountiful lands and waters.

Washington's family, along with other prominent Virginia families, owned shares in the Ohio Company of Virginia which held a grant in the Ohio River Basin. The French government, desiring to shore up its position from the Ohio Valley into French Canada, sent troops to occupy the territory. French Canada, whose population at that time numbered less than sixty thousand farmers, fishermen and fur traders, was also attempting to acquire as yet unsettled land along the

Ohio River. Consequently, under the command of Marquis Abraham Du Quesne, a French Canadian fort stood at the confluence of the Allegheny and Monongahela Rivers, which rivers merge to form the Ohio River.

At age 22, when Washington was commissioned Lieutenant-Colonel of the Virginia Militia, Governor Robert Dinwiddie assigned him to the western frontier. Dinwiddie decided to send English colonial forces into the Ohio Valley with his instructions to the French to depart and he chose Washington to deliver his orders. Accordingly, on November 23, 1753, Lieutenant Colonel George Washington arrived at the French stronghold of Fort Duquesne (originally spelled Du Quesne after the marquis).

Commanding approximately 150 men, Washington encountered a hopeless military situation at the Fort. Though the French proved too intimidating for the Virginia Militia, Washington learned much spiritually and diplomatically during that deployment. Significantly, he acquired invaluable knowledge of guerrilla warfare as practiced by the Native Americans of that region. Such knowledge would later help him to turn the tide of defeat during the Revolutionary War.

The young Virginian instinctively relied on moral force when he encountered difficulties. This endeared him to the Indian leaders of the Ohio Valley whom he met during that deployment. The local Indian "Half King" let it be known that he discerned spiritual greatness in young Washington, and that he trusted him, even though he sometimes called him by the Indian name "Conotocarius," meaning "Devourer of Villages," originally assigned by Half King's tribe to Washington's grandfather two generations earlier.

During the expedition, Washington had a narrow brush with death in the vicinity of the French Fort LeBoeuf, (near Erie, Pennsylvania). As young Washington and an aid took a short cut through dense woods, they came upon a party of French Indians who ambushed them. One of the prowling Indians fired directly at Washington's chest. Washington said of the incident that he was "not fifteen steps off......"[74] A story survives that the bullets did not harm Washington at that close range. He merely brushed gun powder off his uniform while the firing Indian instantly fell to his knees to worship the giant his shotgun would not kill. Without hesitation, young George, ever a man of humor and quick wit, reached forward and lifted the quaking warrior to his feet. "I am a man just like you," he reassured the frightened Indian.

Washington wrote further of the incident.

"We took this fellow into custody...Then let him go and walked all the remaining part of the night."[75]

Washington's superior rank allowed him to over-rule his aide who insistently demanded that the Indian be killed lest he follow them and complete his lethal work.

Though Washington had delivered Governor Dinwiddie's instructions to the French commandant, the Chevalier de St. Pierre, he met with no success. Washington's reports to Governor Dinwiddie on French plans, arms and Indian alliances however, were so impressive that the Governor rushed them into print for attention not only in the colonies, but also in London.

By spring of 1755, the aristocratic Major General Edward Braddock, Commander-in-Chief of the King of

England's North American Forces, commissioned young
George Washington Captain of North American Forces,
the highest position he had authority to fill in the colonies.
Washington, by now highly familiar with the terrain and
dangers imposed by the untamed wilderness beyond
Western Maryland, explained the perils of a military expe-
dition in that region to General Braddock. The patrician
General summarily dismissed Washington's knowledge and
opinions of the western front. Nonetheless, on May 10,
1755, General Braddock appointed Captain George
Washington his aide de camp. As such, he would accompany
Braddock and his forces in their deployment to capture Fort
Duquesne and open the Western lands.

The hardship of the march over the Allegheny
Mountains far exceeded the expectations of the English
General. He had under-estimated the distance, harshness of
the land, cruelty of the weather and steep difficulties of the
mountains. Supply wagons simply could not haul their
loads. Mud and rains joined their fury to stall the British
military march.

Along the way, Captain Washington providentially
became quite ill. Bloody dysentery, perhaps from polluted
water, infected many of the soldiers. Not to be deterred,
Braddock decided to send a single detachment supported by
artillery ahead to Fort Duquesne. Young Washington desper-
ately longed to be among the regiment who would plant the
flag of England on French soil at Fort Duquesne; instead, sick
with dysentery, fever, pain and weakness, he remained con-
fined to his cot. Debilitating illness continued to keep George
prostrate in the back of a wagon until a physician had the

presence of mind to administer a patent medicine that gradually alleviated Washington's problem. He then proceeded in
the back of a moving wagon toward the front. Messages
abounded of Indian massacres, colonial families being
scalped and slain. Still too weak to ride horseback, George
continued toward the front by covered wagon.

The possibility of participating in the liberation of Fort
Duquesne drove Washington's valiant efforts in crossing the
rough terrain to the battle site. The military plan was to
transport troops, artillery and wagons across the
Monongahela River and on to victory at the nearby Fort.
George was twenty-three years old, unaccustomed to weakness, yet powerless over his physical problem. As he neared
the battle front, he worried that he could not endure the jolts
of a warrior horse.

Captain Washington's job required him to be mounted
and afield at the charge on Fort Duquesne. Severe dysentery
causes certain rawness. To lessen his pain, Washington pro-
cured several pillows and tied them to his saddle. Little did he
know then how this fortuity would save his life[76] and help to
launch his luminous legend.

The English militia had never before fought a coalition of
Indians and French using guerrilla tactics. General Braddock
continued to disregard young Washington's experienced
counsel about warfare on the Western frontier. His royal
troops were untrained to fight an enemy they could not see.
Suddenly, war hoops from invisible warriors they had never
before heard chilled their veins. The terrified British soldiers
broke ranks. Into this mayhem rode General Braddock,

accompanied by his aid de camp George Washington perched high on his pillow-laden saddle.

The brutal battle quickly escalated into fierce combat. George somehow managed to stay in his saddle despite his pain and weakness, thanks in no small part to the pillows upon which he sat. His tall 6' 4" figure was an easy mark for the hidden riflemen. When his horse was shot out from under him, Washington found another, remounted, pillows and all, and made his way to the front. A second time his horse was shot from under him, and he again found another to mount. An unseen rifleman fired at his face and pierced his hat. Two more bullets scorched through his hat. But Washington rode on, seated high on his pillows and focusing on his job. Then, hot lead pierced his uniform, but he remained untouched. Eyewitnesses were both stunned and frightened. The myth of invincible George Washington, an American Achilles, was born during that battle. In Washington's words:

> "By the all powerful dispensations of Providence, I have been protected beyond all human probability or expectation, for I had four bullets through my coat, and two horses shot under me, yet escaped unhurt, although death was leveling my companions on every side of me."[77]

Suddenly, General Braddock fell to the ground as bullets crashed through his right arm and penetrated his lung. Fiendish whoops of the savages frightened Braddock's soldiers even more and led them to panic. Washington quickly responded. His job was to take his fallen Commander-in-Chief across the river and out of the line of fire. He commandeered a small wagon to transport the severely wounded Major General. Under intense fire, Washington personally conveyed his suffering leader across the ford.

Indians pounced onto the battlefield and competed with vultures to plunder the dead, scalp the wounded and rob the wagons. Perceiving this atrocity, Braddock commanded Washington to rally the men who were fleeing in every direction. By nightfall, retreat was the only possibility. Though Washington had been on horseback for more than twelve hours, Braddock ordered him to guide the retreat. Moral courage was George Washington's solution to the physically impossible. After more than twenty-four consecutive hours of battle waged on horseback, Washington's weary horse carried him back to camp the morning of July 10.

Braddock, in the meantime, was transported by cart, and then transferred to a hand litter. When his spent men refused to carry him further, he mounted a horse and led the exhausted, frightened men back to camp. Braddock died on July 13, praising the gallantry and good conduct of his officers and deploring the bad behavior of the men.[78] Washington personally buried the British General with as much military dignity as the situation could afford. He made certain that no enemy Indians would discover the grave and desecrate the body of the fallen leader.

Later George Washington would say of his highly criticized deceased Commanding Officer:

"General Braddock was unfortunate, and his character was much too severely treated. He was one of the honestest and best men of the British officers with whom I was acquainted; even in manner of fighting he was not more to blame than others."[79]

George, as soon as his health improved, headed back to Virginia to his beloved Mount Vernon. He had overheard the laments of soldiers who believed they had been led into the wilderness to be slaughtered. The consensus of thinking men of the time was that General Braddock had been overconfident in an unfamiliar country where warfare was different in every way from what he knew and for which he was trained.

Subsequently, young Washington, in spite of or perhaps because of the legend of his excellence, was unjustly humiliated by his superiors in endeavors surrounding the Ohio Valley military campaign and the French and Indian War. This was a clear and painful purification for the brilliant young soldier. George Washington's officers however, offered the following tribute to their twenty-six-year-old leader:

"[H]e was the only man able to support 'the military character of Virginia', a chieftain who could by example 'inculcate those genuine sentiments of true honor and passion for glory from which the greatest military achievements have been derived.'"[80]

Washington remained in charge of Virginia's chain of border forts which protected colonists from Indian raids. He

tamed the wilderness, recruited and trained militia, and gar-
nered supplies and funds to support his troops. By 1758,
London sent General John Forbes to conquer Fort Duquesne
and liberate the Western lands for the British crown. No
longer a sick youth, but a tested warrior, Colonel Washington
and his Virginia regiment had by November, moved to within a one day ride of Fort Duquesne. They intended to camp
there until spring, when they would launch a full scale attack
on the Fort and oust the French once and for all. Then, as
luck would have it, a few prisoners fell into their hands, from
whom they learned how weak and disabled the fortifications
of the Fort actually were.

Wasting no time, Washington and his men achieved the
victory he had so fervently prayed for in the back of the con-
voy wagon two years earlier. His joy was complete as he salut-
ed the raising of the British flag at Fort Duquesne. He wrote
of the victory to Virginia Governor Francis Fauquier:

> "I have the pleasure to inform you that Fort
> Duquesne, or the ground rather on which it stood,
> was possessed by his Majesty's troops on the 25th
> instant. The enemy...burned the fort and ran away
> at night (by its light)."[81]

In 1758, believing his military career over, twenty-six-
year-old Washington resigned his rank and retired to Mount
Vernon. The officers who served with him were deeply disap-
pointed and wrote to him: "In our earliest Infancy, you took
us under your Tuition, train'd us up in the practice of that
Discipline which alone can constitute good Troops."[82] They

bewailed the "loss of such an excellent Commander, such a sincere friend, and so affable a companion."[83]

Washington now passed hours each day studying the Bible. Hunting was a favorite pastime. He also enjoyed learned conversation with his refined, hospitable neighbor George Mason. Washington frequently traveled by horseback through the vast untamed forests and wildernesses of Virginia, Maryland and Pennsylvania. Sixteen years after the great Battle of the Monongahela, in 1772, Washington and a colleague, Dr. James Craik, were traveling through the Ohio Valley with a group of hunters on a business trip. They were visited by an Indian tribe, whose aged Chief, of lofty stature and offering a dignified and imposing appearance, showed reverential deference to Colonel Washington. When night fell and shadows of the camp fire were bright, the aged Chief rose from his meditation to address the group. He bowed to George Washington with immense respect while his interpreter translated the Indian Chief's prophesy:

"I am chief and ruler over my tribes. My influence extends to the waters of the great lakes and to the far Blue Mountains. I have traveled a long and weary path, that I might see the young warrior of the great battle. It was on the day when the white man's blood mixed with the streams of our forest, that I first beheld this chief. I called to my young men and said, mark yon tall and daring warrior? He is not of the red coat tribe—he hath an Indian's wisdom, and his warriors fight as we do—himself alone is exposed. Quick, let your aim be certain and he dies. Our rifles were leveled, rifles which, but for him, knew not how to miss—'twas all in vain, a power mightier far than we, shielded him from harm. He cannot die in battle. I am old, and soon shall be gathered to the great council fire of my fathers in the land of shades, but ere I go, there is something bids me speak in the voice of prophecy. Listen! The Great Spirit protects that man, and guides his destinies—he will become the chief of nations, and a people yet unborn will hail him as the founder of a mighty empire."[84]

CHAPTER FIVE

Washington's Leadership

"...[T]he ways of Providence are inscrutable, and
Mortals must submit."
—George Washington

T hough History recounts little of Washington's childhood, family challenges nourished seeds of leadership
in Washington's character. Biographer Ferling observes:

"Nowhere in his vast correspondence does
Washington reveal his feelings about his youth,
other than to say that his parents sought to raise him
so that he would never be 'in danger of becoming
indolent ...imperious & dissipated'.[86] ...After 1743,
when George was on the cusp of adolescence, [his
mother] lived alone with her children at Ferry Farm,
a worn-out tract near Fredericksburg. Contem-
poraries describe her as quiet, aloof, imperious, and
strong-willed. She frightened some youngsters, who

saw her as regal and omnipotent. ... [I]t was in part from her that George derived his Olympian public persona of the quiet, stately, august individual ...Washington's subsequent behavior suggests that he honored, and perhaps deeply loved, his mother."[87]

Eleven-year-old George would have been the delight of his mother's heart as the new widow struggled to build a life for herself and her six fatherless children. Because she was a woman, she had no legal rights. Her eldest son held her legal fate. One can only imagine the fear Mary Washington had to overcome as she emerged from the graveyard of her recently deceased husband to face her needy children. Her Bible was her authority: her faith was the rock upon which she parented. Whatever Mary Washington did in those few years after the death of her husband, she raised a son steeped in elegance, clothed in humility, and endowed with physical and emotional strength beyond telling.

Washington's leadership skills were finely honed during his late teenage years when he left his mother's home and came to live with his half-brother Lawrence who "...associated with the most powerful men in the province and with the most sophisticated women that George had ever seen. Dashing, confident, polished, valorous, and not least the object of apparently heart-felt reverence and adulation, Lawrence was everything...."[88]

George Washington however, as he reached early manhood, became the source of emotional and psychological support for Lawrence, who contracted terminal tuberculosis. Helping his beloved elder brother as he withered and died was an experience in God's ways that George Washington's faith was powerful enough to withstand.

On July 3, 1775, when he was unanimously appointed to lead the Continental Army in dangerous and difficult circumstances, Washington's army was the laughing stock of England. His childhood training had effectively prepared him for the moment. As Washington assumed command in the shade of an elm tree near the campus of Harvard College in Cambridge, Massachusetts, his men were poorly trained, poorly equipped and would rarely be paid. They were about to "...tangle with the largest expeditionary force sent forth in the eighteenth century."[89] There was, however, a breathtaking promise of victory in the air that few could disregard. Three months earlier, young Patrick Henry had stood at the pulpit of Saint John's Church in Richmond, Virginia shouting, "Give me liberty or give me death!" Those words were an electric current in the colonies that few understood at the time though all were seared by their power.

History affirms the single-handed courage of George Washington as he shouldered the challenge of establishing America's independence. His leadership in the break with England inaugurated a Herculean precedent that America's true spirit is sacrificial love, the only authentic love. He had acquired that soul skill at the knee of his grieving mother at Ferry Farm. America's spirit gives life, breeds prosperity that sustains life and nourishes peace that ennobles life. As historian Fred Anderson said of George Washington:

> "Great as the perils that faced him in 1776 were, and as long as the odds against success seemed as twenty-

five thousand redcoats backed by the most powerful fleet on earth prepared to attack his much smaller army, there is no indication that Washington worried much about what, precisely his destiny might be. There would have been little point in doing so, for as he explained much later, 'the great ruler of events' alone knew the purpose of whatever happened on earth. Therefore, he believed, 'we safely trust the issue to him, without perplexing ourselves to seek for that which is beyond human ken; only taking care to perform the parts assigned us, in a way that reason and our own conscience approve of.' It was an austere faith, but a real one. His duty lay before him. That was enough."[90]

General Washington was observed by others as a distinguished man who inspired admiration and commitment to nobler aspirations among his associates. One of his colleagues, Benjamin Latrobe remarked:

"There is something uncommonly commanding and majestic in his walk, his address, his figure and his countenance."[91]

Though his appearance was stately, even regal, Washington's thoughts and concerns included, as Joseph J. Ellis observed: "men shedding blood."[92]   Washington, no stranger to poverty, sickness and death led a motley bunch; those who came from "the lowest rung of American society."[93] The Continental Army was staffed by "indentured servants, former slaves, landless sons, and recent immigrants

"History has canonized George Washington as the most esteemed of the Founding Fathers for many reasons. Without his transfiguring faith, personal self-sacrifice, expertise and, most significantly of all, victory on the battlefield, the Declaration of Independence would have been a seal of defeat and certain death for the signers."

5   "As Washington assumed command...near the campus of Harvard College in Cambridge, Massachusetts, his men were poorly trained, poorly equipped and would rarely be paid. They we about to '...tangle with the largest expeditionary force sent forth in the eighteenth century.'"

6   "Washington...said that his triumphs at Trenton and Princeton proceeded from good fortune. He knew that fortune favors the brave and the bold. He also knew, adored, and obeyed the Divine Source of good fortune."

from Ireland and England. These were young men, usually between fifteen and twenty-five years of age...and signed on 'for the duration' of the war because, in most cases, they had no brighter prospects."[94] They saw in their Commander-in-Chief a distinguished leader who resonated with their hopes and dreams.

Washington, highly esteemed by his men, was quite capable of exerting manly authority over them, even to extremes. Biographer Ellis observed: "He [Washington] was prepared to string them up if they attempted to desert or fell asleep on sentinel duty, and order one hundred lashes to their backs for minor infractions."[95] In spite of his fury, which few wished to incite, Washington was sincerely venerated by his Army. "The soldiers were known to chant the sing-songy tune 'War and Washington' so endlessly that visiting civilians complained."[96] The troops knew he needed them and that was enough.

General Washington and his soldiers shared a decided commitment to one another. The men saw a glimpse of themselves in their leader. He too had everything to lose if the war was lost, and having the reputation of being the richest man in Virginia, he in fact had much more to lose than anyone else in his army. Necessity was the staying power of the Continental Army. Sacrificial commitment was the glue that held them together. Biographer James Thomas Flexner said of Washington:

"...[F]rom the moment of his command, Washington was more than a military leader; he was the eagle, the standard, the flag, the living symbol of the cause."[97] And "In all history, few men who possessed unassailable power have used that power so gently and self-effacingly for what their best instincts told them was the welfare of their neighbor and all mankind."[98]

Biographer M. E. Bradford said of General George Washington's leadership:

"Certainly Washington looked the part of commander-in-chief—almost six feet, four inches tall, and about two hundred pounds, athletic, and with the eye and bearing of a general."[99]

Biographer John R. Alden described Washington as a

"well mannered, quiet and impressive man with the military bearing. …There was about him an aura of power, determination, dignity and probity that impressed everyone."[100]

Abigail Adams, wife of the Second President of the United States described Washington as being

"…[P]olite with dignity, affable without familiarity, distant without haughtiness, grave without austerity, modest, wise and good."[101]

Bradford described the man.

"Washington was no 'man of the people' to be clapped on the shoulder. In moments of seriousness his formality was severe and aristocratic—the product of a code developed under the old regime in Virginia. Yet he was a republican in the classic sense, and altogether in character when he declared: 'The approbation and affection of a free people [are] the greatest earthly rewards.'"[102]

George Washington withstood adversity with as much dignity as his modesty allowed him to welcome success. On May 2, 1778, amid the deprivation and desolation of Valley Forge, as Commander-in-Chief of the starving, pitiful revolutionary forces, General Washington encouraged his troops to ascend to the pinnacles of self-sacrifice for the good of others. He issued an order at Headquarters, Valley Forge, May 2, 1778, in which he asked them to consider the following:

"In addition to the distinguished character of a Patriot, it should be our highest glory to add the more distinguished character of a Christian."[103]

The Continental Army was indeed a sacred structure unto itself. General Washington had set the course of his life and the revolutionary battles directly within the framework of the providential love of God the Father. Of course, the troops looked to him in his religious dimension. Washington was an icon of Christian fortitude and fairness for his army.

His indomitable faith in the kindness of Divine Providence and the righteousness of America's cause are evident in historian Barbara W. Tuchman's description of the conditions he faced as Commander-in-Chief during the winter, 1779–1780 at Morristown, New Jersey.

"Rations were reduced for already hungry men who had been shivering in the snows to one-eighth of normal quantities. Two leaders of a protest by Connecticut regiments demanding full rations and back pay were hanged to quell an uprising. In January, 1781, Pennsylvania regiments mutinied and, with troops of New Jersey, deserted to the number of half their strength before the outbreak was suppressed. At the frontiers, Indians out of the woods guided by Loyalists were burning farms and massacring civilians. Even to keep an army in the field was problematical, because soldiers of the militia had to be furloughed to go home to harvest their crops, and if leave were refused, they would desert. Fighting a war in such circumstances, said General von Steuben, the army's Prussian drillmaster, 'Caesar and Hannibal would have lost their reputations.'"[104]

Washington valued his troops and they knew it. He asked much of them. The General expected their lives, like his, to be poured out on behalf of their fellow citizens. He suffered with them, and triumphed with them. In April of

1778, Washington wrote the following to John Bannister about his army.

> "...[N]o Order of Men in the Thirteen States have paid a more sanctimonious regard to their proceedings than the Army; and, indeed it may be questioned, whether there has been that scrupulous adherence to them by any other, for without arrogance, or the smallest deviation from truth, it may be said that no history now extant can furnish an instance of an Army's suffering such uncommon hardships as ours have done, and bearing them with the same patience and Fortitude. To see men without clothes to cover their nakedness, without blankets to lay on, without shoes, by which their marches might be traced by the blood from their feet, and almost as often without provisions as with; marching through frost and snow, and at Christmas taking up their Winter Quarters within a day's march of the enemy, without a house or hut to cover them til they could be built, and submitting to it without a murmur, is a mark of patience and obedience which in my opinion can scarce be paralleled."[105]

George Washington entwined love of country with the highest goals of the human character. A truly Christian man, he inspired citizens to the heights of sacrifice out of love for their country, for their families and for one another. He nourished the root of American patriotism with his belief that God creates human beings in His own image and likeness.

Washington never wavered in his faith that Kind Providence loves His people and wills only the best for each.

Wisdom generously endowed Washington with vision to see truth. Leaders great and small need that gift. He continuously experienced the earth as a testing ground. Knowledge unveiled many secrets to Washington: why humans exist, why the Creator of all that is seen and unseen bothered to create humans, and what they are to do with their lives. Understanding revealed that Kind Providence sends humans to the earth to know Him as He allows, love Him as He deserves, serve Him as He desires, and to love and serve one another for Him, with Him and in Him. Such individual reciprocity of love and service brings humans into personal harmony with Kind Providence in their ascent to the heights of human development.

The troops, the Continental Congress represented by John Adams, liaison for matters of war, and the citizens of the colonies struggling for freedom willingly rallied around General Washington as their symbol. George Washington, leader that he was, gave external expression to his internal acts of religion. He shared with others in religious matters and he professed his religion on the national stage in visual community. He allowed his religious dimension to shine for all to see. He was however, never one of those who act or pray "that they may be seen by men."[106] He preferred to commune with God in private.[107] George Washington was raised up by Kind Providence on the shoulders of colonial Americans to exhibit for all of them the truth of religious freedom expressed through loving deeds for humanity as a fundamental, individual right. He is justly called the champion of religious liberty.

The Revolutionary War included death-riddled battles on many fronts. They were gruesome as are all battles. George Washington and his troops, however, were fighting for a higher purpose than their self. General Washington was more than Commander-in-Chief of the Continental Army. He was the man-servant of Congress, a civil authority of men representing the will of the people who elected them. Their mandate was to create conditions favorable to fostering authentic Judaic-Christian religious life from which they believed their personal and real property rights flow. That principle (of property ownership) resides in a people fulfilling their spiritual duties, thereby ennobling society at large with moral qualities of justice and peace everyone understands. Washington's wisdom envisioned a nation of people whose behavior would be sourced in faithfulness to the loving plan of Kind Providence for all people governed. Therein lies governmental legitimacy. George Washington's public life of leadership, his subsequent retirement at Mount Vernon, and the circumstances of his death (described in Chapter Nine) disclose that he understood wisdom's moral imperative exquisitely. His success is only as valuable as each succeeding generation of Americans elect leaders who refine and implement the moral imperatives he so brilliantly planted.

George Washington, a realist, consistently embraced truth as his shield and banner. After his death, Abigail Adams said of him: "Simple truth is his best, his greatest eulogy. She alone can render his fame immortal." George

Washington was deeply aware of America's unique origin at the confluence of the tides of history and heroism.[108] His personal acuity, prayer life, fortitude, commitment and discipline allowed him to receive and administer vast amounts of divine wisdom.[109] George Washington was a man who valued principle above all else in his personal life, on the battlefield and in public service.[110] His success solidified the inalienable rights of every law abiding citizen. He welcomed wisdom as his guide at the Constitutional Conventions. Knowledge pursued him in his deliberations as first President of the United States. Understanding upheld him in his dedication to the responsibilities inherent in the ownership of private property. Fortitude carried him from the depths of sorrow to the heights of glory. Washington never took honor for himself. No true citizen does. Washington's spiritual journey reveals that his life, lived for a higher purpose than mere self, is eternal. Paradoxically, few men tasted more peace or exhibited more joy in life than the great warrior President. He was a peacemaker in the widest sense of the word. Washington believed that peace and joy find and dwell with those who are faithful to the highest ideals of Kind Providence.

Washington prayed for guidance; to know God's ways and respond fully. His men knew that about him; his faith was strong enough for all of them. Washington trusted that in God's Plan for humanity, all things, ideas, goals and achievements work together for just peace. Thanks in large measure to George Washington's influence on the Founders, life, liberty and the pursuit of happiness is the birthright and endowment of law abiding Americans. There is value to harvest now in an analysis of George Washington's leadership sourced in his spiritual life. Though certain Indians of Western Pennsylvania and even the less enlightened of his troops and constituencies may have perceived him as a deity, Washington aggressively repudiated such claims and identified himself simply as a servant of the Republic. His name was honored throughout America and in the courts of Europe, yet he presented himself merely as a beneficiary of God's mercy and a servant of the governed in a land where authentic love and just peace are possible.

America's Founding Father is not distinguished as a military genius. Yet he was. He is not esteemed as a landed aristocrat, though he was master of vast territory. Washington is not a literary giant, but his words dazzle the mind of every free person. It is the noble spirit of George Washington that hovers over America. Beloved as a sacrificial citizen, commander-in-chief, first President of the United States and Christian gentleman, George Washington is America's mystical icon of heroic grace. U.S. News and World Report, in a Special Collector's Edition published in September of 2002 reported:

"George Washington's character made him something of an exception to the dominant political style. He held more truly to the ideal of disinterested, principled, and non-partisan leadership than any other founding brother. (Maybe, in his case, the sobriquet of father is just.) ...Although he could be stern, hot tempered, and unforgiving as deserters from the Continental Army learned with their lives, he was unfailingly a man of principle."[111]

George Washington cautioned against human hubris and that injunction remains as valid today as ever. He warned that those who seek glory for themselves are robbers. All honor, glory and power belong to God our Father who art in Heaven. When he took the oath of office as the first (and only) unanimously elected President of the United States at Federal Hall in New York City on April 30, 1789, Washington improvised "So help me God" at the conclusion of the first presidential oath and kissed the Bible.[112] "No historian would be well advised to depict Washington as anything other that a sincere Christian."[113] He lived the Gospel.

Washington prayed often that he might adhere to God's loving plan for his life of service to his new nation. He struggled to remain faithful to Kind Providence's loving, though all too often challenging ways. After his appointment as Commander-in Chief of the Continental forces, he confided to his wife: "You may believe me, my dear, when I assure you, in the most solemn manner, that so far as seeking this appointment, I have used every endeavor to avoid it..." From the beginning, he entreated all Americans to respond to the graced spirit of sacrificial duty for God and country. In 1775, he spoke to his newly assembled Army, telling the troops:

> "...[You] are now the Troops of the United Provinces of North America; and it is hoped that all distinctions of Colonies will be laid aside; so that one and the same spirit may animate the whole, and the only contest be, who shall render, on this great

and trying occasion, the most essential service to the great and common cause in which we are engaged."

Consider George Washington's prayer that grew out of a closing paragraph of his letter to the governors of the thirteen states on the occasion of his retirement from command of the Continental Army:

"I now make it my earnest prayer, that God would have you and the State over which you preside, in His holy protection, that He would incline the hearts of the citizens to cultivate a spirit of subordination and obedience to Government, to entertain a brotherly affection and love for one another, for their fellow citizens of the United States at large, and particularly for their brethren who have served in the Field [the military], and finally that He would most graciously be pleased to dispose us all to do Justice, to love mercy, and to demean ourselves with that Charity, humility and pacific temper of mind, which were the Characteristics of the Divine Author of our blessed Religion [Judeo-Christianity], and without an humble imitation of whose example in these things, we can never hope to be a happy Nation."[114]

In 1783, at a critical moment for the military and the Congress of the new nation, General Washington, whose faith in his troops and his country never wavered, grave and "agitated" according to an observer, stood before the victorious Continental army. Biographer John Ferling describes the scene.

> "Men hurried to their seats. Washington waited patiently until the scraping of chairs and all commotion ceased. When the room fell totally silent, he slowly unfolded a sheaf of papers, looked up one last time, then gazed at his notes and began to read. The men strained to hear him...He told the officers that he had been with them since the first, and that he had never left their side, save for times when Congress called him away. He spoke lovingly of the army, and of how his reputation was inextricably tied to it. ...He closed his prepared address by asking the officers to remember 'your sacred honor,' your country, the 'natural character of America,' and the 'rights of humanity.' He paused. Not a sound was heard in the great room. Slowly he reached again in his pocket. He extracted a pair of glasses, and slowly put them on. The men had never seen General Washington in spectacles. Looking over his glasses at the packed room, Washington begged their indulgence at his wearing glasses. In a soft voice that resonated with anger, fatigue, and unbridled despair, he told the officers: "Gentlemen, you must pardon me. I have grown gray in your service and now find myself growing blind. ...Throughout the hall, men were weeping, tough men who had witnessed much

carnage and had grown accustomed to life-and-death decisions…"[115]

Unquestionably, George Washington would always be their leader for sacrificial love knows no bounds.

George Washington's more than two-hundred-year-old America is a youth with many choices: George Washington's survival rule for America is "one nation undivided under God." Prayer is a sign of America's kinship with God. George Washington Parke Curtis wrote of General Washington, his step-grandfather:

"Throughout the war, as it was understood in his military family, he gave a part of every day to private prayer and devotion."[116]

Growing pains are real. George Washington knew the meaning of life on earth and in the hereafter.[117] His response to such knowledge was prayer, both personal and private, as well as public. He wrote the following about each citizen's spiritual responsibilities:

"Of all the animosities which have existed among mankind, those which are caused by a difference of sentiments in religion appear to be the most inveterate and distressing, and ought to be deprecated. I was in hopes that the enlightened and liberal policy, which has marked the present age, would at least have reconciled Christians of every denomination so far that we should never again see the religious disputes carried to such a pitch as to endanger the peace of society."[118]

George Washington experienced Earth as the testing ground for eternal life. The mere fact that this book about his spiritual journey exists for us to ponder is indisputable evidence that his spirit lives on to invigorate, challenge and guide us in the twenty-first century. Hard-fought-for liberty and vigilant justice for law abiding citizens are rewards worth cherishing. The Founding Father wrote:

"I had always hoped that this land might become a safe and agreeable Asylum to the virtuous and persecuted part of mankind, to whatever nation they might belong."[119]

Domestic tranquility has a price. In 1791, Congress passed an excise tax on whiskey to help pay national debts. Of course, western grain farmers protested violently and by 1794, the protesters numbered nearly six thousand angry men gathered at Braddock Field in Pittsburgh. President Washington was deeply troubled by the civil unrest in France that eventually led to the bloody French Revolution, and saw its destructive seeds in the armed uprising in Pennsylvania. His goal as President was to protect the fledgling infant nation against all odds and nurture it into steadfast strength. George Washington once again mounted his mighty white horse in full battle dress, and personally commanding a national force of thirteen thousand men, the sitting American President led his troops as far as Carlisle,

Pennsylvania. With such a show of force, the rebels dispersed and national interests trumped regional grievances. Washington offered amnesty to all rebels who signed an oath to obey the federal government.

In 1793, when England and France went to war against each other, President Washington was careful to hold the course for neutrality, thereby giving the baby nation breathing space to grow and mature. Thomas Jefferson, younger than Washington and an outspoken Francophile was an opponent of the first President on certain issues. Yet he too, speaking for those who would disagree with the first President, identified George Washington as "…the one man who outweighs them all in influence over all the people."

Executive branch precedents created by President Washington have stood the test of time. Washington's leadership was a reconciling force that brought harmony to America, her allies and enemies alike, revealing pure and benign light of Revelation that has a meliorating influence on mankind and increases the blessings of all.[120] History teaches that good eventually triumphs over evil in the life of mankind. Washington cautioned in his Circular to the States:

"…[T]he United States came into existence as a Nation, and if their citizens should not be completely happy, the fault will be entirely their own."

CHAPTER SIX

Washington's Faith

"The time is now near at hand which must probably determine whether Americans are to be freemen or slaves; whether they are to have any property they can call their own: whether their houses and farms are to be pillaged and destroyed, and themselves consigned to a state of wretchedness from which no human efforts will deliver them. The fate of unborn millions will now depend, under God, on the courage and conduct of this army. Our cruel and unrelenting enemy leaves us only the choice of brave resistance, or the most abject submission. We have, therefore, to resolve to conquer or die."[121]

—General George Washington's Address to the Continental Army before the Battle of Long Island, August 27, 1776

*G*eorge Washington's leadership won the war that set Americans free. His faith carried him through every tribulation. No other explanation suffices. Washington, convinced that religion and morality are the essential pillars of civil society, led by example, rarely by words. History is clear that Washington was keenly aware of his moral and religious duties. He intuitively knew that no one fully understands the mysterious ways of God. Though he was a life-long Christian, General Washington never imposed his personal faith on anyone. The record is unambiguous that he respected everyone's belief as a sacred, God-given personal trust. He wanted everyone in the new nation, of all faiths, and even those of no faith to feel welcome, involved and committed to the highest ideals of legitimate government flowing from the people, for the people, by the people and of the people. George Washington began his presidency by spelling out the responsibilities of citizens of diverse faith traditions in the new nation.

Like many Christians of the times, Roman Catholics were no strangers to persecution and intolerance. By 1789, they were dispersed throughout the thirteen states. On March 15 of that year, Washington wrote a memo to the Roman Catholics in the United States:

> "...As mankind becomes more liberal, they will be more apt to allow that all those who conduct themselves as worthy members of the community [of whatever religious belief] are equally entitled to the protection of civil government. I hope ever to see

America among the foremost nations in examples of justice and liberality."[122]

Two months later, in May, 1789, Washington presented the following to the United Baptist Churches of Virginia:

"I beg you will be persuaded that no one would be more zealous than myself to establish effectual barriers against the horrors of spiritual tyranny, and every other species of religious persecution... Every man, conducting himself as a good citizen and being accountable to God alone for his religious opinions, ought to be protected in worshipping the Deity according to the dictates of his own conscience."[123]

That same month, in May of 1789, he expressed to the General Assembly of Presbyterian Churches:

"I desire you to accept my acknowledgements of your laudable endeavors to render men sober, honest, and good Citizens, and the obedient subjects of a lawful government."[124]

In August of 1789, President Washington personally addressed representatives of the Hebrew Congregation of Newport, Rhode Island. The following statement articulates Washington's deeply held convictions about the American doctrine of separation of Church and State.

"The citizens of the United States of America have a right to applaud themselves for having given to mankind...a policy worthy of imitation. All possess alike liberty of conscience, and immunities of citizenship. It is now no more that toleration is spoken of, as if it was by the indulgence of one class of people, that another enjoyed the exercise of their inherent natural rights. For happily the government of the United States, which gives to bigotry no sanction—to persecution no assistance, requires only that they who live under its protection should demean themselves as good citizens, in giving it on all occasions their effectual support."[125]

Washington was uniquely renowned throughout the world of his time as a humble man of God. He set the precedents for the distinction between public and private religion in the United States that underlie the First Amendment guarantee of separation of Church and state. He was well aware of the devastation wrought upon decent, God-fearing people by religious wars and persecutions based on spiritual beliefs. The horrors and anarchy of the French Revolution were never far from his mind. His goal for the United States was to adhere strictly to the doctrine of separation of church and state. He had little use for pseudo piety. He believed a person's worth is judged only by his deeds. He expected decent people to do decent things for one another. He held leaders to high standards. In 1789, he wrote:

"Government being, among other purposes, instituted to protect the consciences of men from oppression, it certainly is the duty of Rulers, not only to abstain from it themselves, but according to their stations, to prevent it in others."

Washington's personal faith was intimately tied to his self-worth and self-esteem. The more weighed down with life's challenges he was, the more humility before man and God became a fiber of his soul. Humility is not an external characteristic: humility is a mark of man's relationship with God. Humility cannot be ascertained with the senses: humility is a condition of the soul. Battle tested and politically savvy, George Washington knew he was totally dependent upon Kind Providence for his next breath.

Like Abraham, his father in faith, Washington obeyed his well-formed conscience: he believed that those who obey God's scriptural plan for the human race reestablish order and balance on God's earth. From generation to generation, the Bible defined just ways for Washington's family to bring order and harmony to their circumstances. Consequently, though Washington walked in the Valley of Darkness for a while, as all men do, interior peace was his path and his light. Obviously the great God of Abraham marked him as His own. Because George Washington was filled with tough love, tested faith and bright hope, his light was a beacon for those he served. His life is a witness of God's loving faithfulness. George Washington led, corrected, advised, appointed, oversaw, prayed, lived and died in the uniform of humility.

Humble Washington firmly believed and acted on the principle that one may discern a man's soul only by his deeds.

War is hell.[126] In 1776, George Washington prayerfully led Americans to freedom's safety when hell opened its jaws to devour them and their property. He was not born a hero. He learned the ways of Kind Providence slowly. Washington knew by first hand experience that true freedom is expensive: it comes only from the Hand of God. True freedom from want of any kind is the goal of mankind. Paradoxically, such freedom is always rooted in detachment from any person, place, thing, activity, ideal or goal contrary to the loving Plan of God for creation.

Washington, descendant of a great chain of Anglican Catholic tradition, privately practiced the faith of his ancestors, parents, wife and stepchildren throughout his life. Some of the other founders however, publicly embraced Deism, a reactionary offspring of the Enlightenment. Deists recognized a type of quasi-divine being who made the world, yet left it to its own devices: not omnipotent, perhaps an absentee overlord of sorts, merely "potent enough to get the world going, as it were, and perhaps to sustain it in existence."[127] Some politicians with whom Washington worked, in their struggle to proclaim a theology that would offend no one, became deists by default.

After careful deliberation, buoyed by extraordinary life experiences, George Washington chose to discard a purely secular vision of public life. Rather, he "mixed the secular and the Judeo-Christian style in an almost perfect balance."[128] It is undisputed that Washington believed in and proclaimed the kindness of Divine Providence, God who is active in human history and rewards the just.

Washington was a vestryman in his Anglican Church in Alexandria, Virginia, and attended services frequently. The entry in Washington's diary for June 5, 1772, shows Washington and his neighbor, George Mason, the author of the Virginia Declaration of Rights, busily engaged in parish business. They made arrangements for church repairs, including replacement of church steps, painting of the church roof and selling church pews to members as a means of generating church revenue. The minutes of the meeting reveal that Washington and George William Fairfax presented the parish with gold leaf to be used to gild letters on Carved Ornaments on the altar.

George and Martha always received Holy Communion before the revolution. Afterward, however, he was not a regular communicant. It is not known why he stopped receiving Holy Communion, but the practice of Holy Communion was not as frequent in those times as it is today, occurring only four times a year. Perhaps Washington stopped receiving the Holy Eucharist due to the time allotment such communion services required; they usually lasted much of the day. Though Martha remained for the entire day, George usually returned home at the conclusion of the Sunday morning worship service. Worshippers in Washington's era may not have understood the Holy Eucharist in the way it is known today. Unworthiness to receive the Blessed Sacrament was a serious consideration. There is no known information of Washington's thoughts on the matter.

In Washington's era, most Americans, pluralistic as they were, believed in God. Through hard-won experience, Washington was unwavering in his conviction that the United States must remain a place where every citizen is free to worship as his or her conscience requires. Washington's immense gift of wisdom, flowing from his faith tradition, allowed him to appreciate that the Eternal Father's Son, Jesus Christ, ransomed each soul with His own body and blood. Wisdom flowing from personal prayer and life experiences showed Washington the proper use of his choices, which end at biological death. He acknowledged true freedom as life in God; for Washington, all that was not of God, for God and with God was deception. Hypocrisy was contrary to his nature. He found his life's path in the Gospel. His mission was to be a faithful follower of Jesus Christ in his private life, ever respectful of the Eternal Father's revelation time-table for humankind in his public life. Consequently, George Washington had no fear of life or death. His deeds are his Gospel testimony.

Duty forced George Washington to abstain from things and places of the world. He preferred family life at Mount Vernon, but faithful servant that he was, his ways melted into God's plan for the United States. Gradually, in prayer and circumstances he recognized the Eternal Father's Hand, he discerned His ways. Graced discipline led him to the desert of obedience. As a result, success flowed from George Washington's faith-filled hands in a silent, humble and seamless web of victory. George Washington, though he was a visionary who foresaw the future republic and would dedicate his life, his fortune and his sacred honor on its behalf, was a man very much in the world of his times.

Young George liked to dance; he knew the courtly step of Virginia's landed gentry. He had impeccable manners. He was handsome, elegant, gracious and witty. He savored fine food and appreciated excellent wine. He enjoyed the favor of high society and was comfortable in the finest salons of the times. He made himself at home in the wilderness. He was a friend and confidante of Indian leaders and frontiersmen. He always had to work. He witnessed much pain and endured immense anguish in his lifetime. He was not a fool. He knew that suffering would always be with us in the world. Aware that earth is a testing ground, Washington was determined not to miss the time of God's visitation in his life.

The heights of asceticism beckoned to Washington constantly. Scarred by smallpox, as were many of his time, Washington had light blue eyes and brown hair. He was tall, especially for those times, lean and quite athletic. Leaders admired him.[129] They "...discerned superior quality in him." He was a popular youth who frequented social events of the Virginia gentry. George Washington very much enjoyed the company of beautiful, well-mannered ladies. He always appreciated goodness and admired virtue. As a young man, he had hoped to marry the daughter of a prosperous merchant in the Rappahannock Valley, but Betsy Fauntleroy rejected him. Washington quietly accepted this personal failure with peaceful resignation.

The typical Virginia Anglican gentleman of Washington's social stature "believed strongly in the sanctity of private opinions and felt it be rude of one person to inflict his personal views upon others...The Anglican 'way' requires eschewing 'enthusiasm' and avoiding outward displays of piety in favor of understatement and even taciturnity…One overriding purpose is not to give offense. Another is to keep the peace. A third is to preserve maximal space for shared sentiments. In gentlemen, 'devoutness' would seem showy, even boastful; the truly devout man ought to hide his devotion."[130] Washington adhered to these norms almost perfectly.

In spite of his charm and obvious social nature, Washington was a deeply private spiritual man. The prism of history shows the depth of Washington's trust in the love and providential Hand of God in his life. He was forthright in his belief that loving Providence guides human history. Washington was a man of few words. Yet people were drawn to him and felt the warmth of his kindness. Still waters do run deep. Prayer was Washington's friend. Prayer freed his heart from inordinate attachments. Prayer revealed the purpose of his life: to cooperate with the loving guidance of the God of his forefathers. Washington's life discloses that there is much merit for those who cooperate with God's loving plan for mankind. All things of the earth pass away but His Sacred Word. George Washington was a dedicated, life-long student of Biblical revelation:

> "During his residence in Philadelphia, as President of the United States, it was the habit of Washington, winter and summer, to retire to his study at a certain hour every night. He usually did so at nine o'clock…A member of the household observed the President upon his knees at a small table, with a candle and open Bible thereon."[131]

Such behavior is characteristic of George Washington. He had more responsibilities that impacted others than any other person of his era. He truly needed divine guidance. On August 20, 1778, he wrote the following to General Thomas Nelson:

"The Hand of providence has been so conspicuous in all this [Revolutionary War], that he must be worse than an infidel that lacks faith, and more than wicked, that has not gratitude enough to acknowledge his obligations."[132]

Throughout his life, true to his Anglican/Episcopalian faith, Washington assiduously avoided false and pretentious piety. He had little time for foolish myth. He disavowed superstition. This practical characteristic ennobled him to his colleagues and foes alike. Washington relied on the Gospel promises of Jesus whose Heart is filled with love for God's poor, sinful children. He trusted Christ the Savior of the world, the Prince of Peace, the source of authentic freedom on earth. Washington, all too often called to forgo his own comfort and pleasure, lived as if there is no tomorrow for anyone. Rather, as he would remind his troops, his colleagues and family, there is only and always the Eternal Now. Life experience taught him that lesson from an early age.

Washington's personal sense of freedom and self-worth rested in his relationship with the great God of Abraham. Early in 1799, the year of his death, he wrote of himself to Bryan Fairfax:

"The favorable sentiments which others, you say, have been pleased to express respecting me, cannot but be pleasing to a mind (sic) who always walked on a straight line, and endeavored as far as human frailties, and perhaps strong passions, would enable him, to discharge the relative duties to his Maker and fellow-men, without seeking any indirect or left handed attempts to acquire popularity."[133]

Washington actively sought to accept God's plan for him and his country, and he prayed fervently to follow God's ways. Though Washington was a man who cherished above all else the peace and comfort of home and family, effort, prayer, sacrifice and circumstances raised him up to be successful surveyor, innovative farmer, self taught scholar, prolific writer, loving family man, esteemed leader, victorious warrior, prescient administrator, brilliant diplomat and master of hospitality. He drank deeper of the bitter cup of defeat than most, yet persevered. George Washington remained lowly though at more than six feet without his boots, he stood taller than most men of his day and attained to the heights of leadership. Ironically, the more famous he became, the more widely he was known to be humble and modest. He continuously strove to bring discipline, humor, beauty, courtesy, bounty and prosperity to his family, his fellow citizens, his beloved Mount Vernon, his troops,[134] the city of Alexandria, the Capital, schools, Universities, and the width and breadth of the new nation.[135]

Chief Justice John Marshall, in his contemporary biography of the first president of the United States, noted the path of freedom that Washington traveled:

"Endowed by nature with a sound judgment, and an accurate and discriminating mind, he feared not that laborious attention which made him perfectly master of those subjects, in all their relations, on which he was to decide; and this essential quality was guided by an unvarying sense of moral right, which would tolerate the employment only of those means that would bear the most rigid examination; by a fairness of intention which neither sought nor required disguise; and by a purity of virtue which not only was untainted, but unsuspected."[136]

Washington's early military career forced him to deal with the savagery of Indian raiders against colonial settlers, and such debauchery seared his soul, making him a total realist. He was perceptive of treachery, especially among those unaware of the mercy of God's redeeming love. On October 25, 1755, settlement families near Wills Creek were severely victimized in a classic Cain and Able conflict. Washington saw the unburied bodies of a scalped woman, a small boy and a young man near their burned out farmhouse. His soldiers found three people brained with stakes, scalped and thrown into a fire that only half consumed them. Washington determined that adequate security for settlers who had rightful title to their property was of absolute necessity. He also realized that "Indians are the only match for

Indians."[137] Washington therefore created alliances with friendly Indians that would protect property rights of landowners.

Washington's burning faith in his youth, strengthened and perfected through hardship and sorrow, served him well during his military career, throughout his presidency and retirement. Washington's wisdom, fortitude and courage solidified American political, religious, financial and personal freedom that has flourished for more than two hundred years. He had a keen sense of the powerful relationship between religious freedom that energizes spiritual commitment and financial prosperity. He personally experienced that connection. Washington bequeaths a dazzling legacy of genuine kindliness that goes far beyond condescending tolerance.

Wisdom speaks through Washington's commands to his troops regarding religious beliefs in Canada where they were being deployed.

> "...[A]void all disrespect to or contempt of the Religion of the Country and its ceremonies. Prudence, Policy and a true Christian Spirit will lead us to look with compassion upon the[m].... without insulting them. While we are contending for our own Liberty, we should be very cautions of violating the Rights of Conscience in others, ever considering that God alone is the Judge of the Hearts of Men, and to Him only in this case, they are answerable."[138]

Washington and those he led forged a life of personal freedom and prosperity on the North American continent unique in the world's history. George Washington's spiritual strength stands guard over every person's moral obligation to seek above all "the pure and benign light of Revelation" to make the world "a display of human greatness and felicity."[139]

Faith expressed through loving deeds served youthful George Washington well as he witnessed first hand dark forces of savagery perpetrating deliberate and massive atrocity against lawful inhabitants of private property. He learned as a young man that peace and security are possible but at a price few willingly pay. Washington battled hand-to-hand with terrorism in the wilderness on the frontier. He learned from the Bible the art of dealing with uncertainty. In Washington's lifetime, just government depended on moral Indians and white men working together for the defense of the frontiers. One of his allies was the powerful Indian leader "Half King." Early in his military career, when young Major Washington met Half King, he described this man as

> "...intelligent, vain, brave, as candid as an Indian ever was, and possessed of an unusual knowledge of white men and their method of fighting. When his passion was stirred, Half King would assert that the reason he hated the French (though he later joined forces with them) was that they had killed, boiled and eaten his father. More immediately he had a bitter grudge because of treatment he had recently had...."[140]

Washington befriended the outraged Indian leader and learned much from him.

George Washington's diplomatic style was to remain sober at all times and listen intently.[141] Perhaps that is why he spoke so little. His divine calling was to salvage and nurture the alliance of decent, law abiding people for the common good. In the French, English and Indian conflict over the Ohio Valley and later during the Revolutionary War, the Constitutional Conventions, his Presidency and retirement, Washington adhered assiduously to his highly tested calling.

George Washington wrote his superior from the frontier: "I shall be studious to avoid all disputes that may end to the public prejudice, but as far as I am able, I will inculcate harmony and unanimity."[142] Washington perfected the art of self-sacrifice for a higher purpose than mere self; his leadership displayed that spiritual concept to the entire nation. Since Bunker Hill, self-sacrifice has been the America way.

Washington had a personal relationship with the Eternal Father who intervened in battle, in relationships, in circumstances, to reward the just and punish evil. Washington prayed to "Kind Providence," all knowing, all powerful, slow to anger, quick to forgive, overflowing with love and benevolence toward humans, beginning with his own chosen people. In his Letter to the Hebrew Congregation of the City of Savannah, Georgia, Washington revealed his prayerful belief and hopes:

"May the same wonder-working Deity, who long since delivered the Hebrews from their Egyptian oppressors, planted them in a promised land, whose providential agency has lately been conspicuous in establishing these United States as an independent nation, still continue to water them with the dews of Heaven and make the inhabitants of every denomination participate in the temporal and spiritual blessings of that people whose God is Jehovah."[143]

Americans inherit much from George Washington. The "public religion" of the United States is the Golden Rule.[144] Good citizens take to the streets to give blood, bring food, clothing, medical aid and moral support in time of need. Americans rally to give what they have so that others might live and experience love. In every moment of infamy, good American citizens are one. For more than two hundred years, George Washington's American offspring have acted on the principle that there are no strangers at the foot of the cross. Suffering introduces people to their lofty origin. Good citizens are good samaritans.

Washington's faith in "Kind Providence" reaches through the centuries to remind every freedom-loving person of the sacred duty to route mayhem from the planet. Faithful commitment to daily duty made early Americans targets for a new kind of warfare, hideous in its sleuth, deceit and monstrosity. Ever since, Americans who die at their posts to defend freedom do not die in vain. Kind Providence always brings good out of evil. Sacrifice on the frontier of liberty unmasks segments of the world inhabited by lost souls wallowing in the darkness of lawlessness, steeped in greed, selfishness, avarice, envy, lust and hatred. The perpetrators send their executioners to the four winds but they do not prevail. They never have in the past, not since Cain killed Able.

America's national moral character manifests itself in self-sacrifice. Freedom from terror is expensive but attainable. Washington knew that. Peaceful, just existence comes at a price that is not negotiable. Lives, fortunes and the sacred honor of every peace-loving person are always on the line to preserve liberty under just law. Many have died helping their fallen brothers and sisters. Such love is the sweet nectar of God's presence in the world. Following George Washington's example, true Americans do overcome adversity. It has always been so in the United States.

Washington's faith in the benevolent Fatherhood of God taught him that decent, law abiding people live an eternal commitment to one another. Diverse people and cultures struggle to become a global family. The first President of the United States triumphed on the American moral frontier. Minorities experienced the wisdom of the Founding Father. Washington forged unity out of difference and diversity rather than from commonality of belief and behavior. Sacrifice is the food of heroes.

Liberty under morally just law is not an easy way of life. George Washington brilliantly perceived that if American ideals are to endure and remain a light for the world, American unity as exemplary people of Kind Providence is the uniform of honor. Liberty under just and equitable law is the goal and reward of American citizenship.

Washington never wavered in his belief that all blessings, benefits and prosperity flow from the loving Hand of God. He was assiduously careful to guard and protect the

First Amendment to the Constitution of the United States that he had taken a Presidential oath to uphold: "Congress shall make no law respecting an establishment of religion or prohibiting the free exercise thereof." George Washington set precedents that give life to the First Amendment. Under his firm, principled leadership, the framers of the Constitution "drew a distinct line between church and state.... [T]hey had great confidence in the individual's ability to understand the world and its most fundamental laws through the exercise of his or her reason. ...[T]he framers sought to secure their idea of religious freedom by barring any alliance between church and state."[145]

Desiring only the best for good citizens, deeply respecting America's pluralistic population, George Washington firmly and unabashedly enjoined moral righteousness as a non-negotiable requirement for everyone who expected to be a citizen of the United States of America. He exercised his freedom of religious belief as a national example when He wrote to the Presbyterian Church General Assembly on May 26, 1789:

"While I reiterate the professions of my dependence upon Heaven as the source of all public and private blessings; I will observe that the general prevalence of piety, philanthropy, honesty, industry, and economy seems, in the ordinary course of human affairs, particularly necessary for advancing and confirming the happiness of our country. While all men within our territories are protected in worshipping the Deity according to the dictates of their consciences;

it is rationally to be expected from them in return, that they will be emulous of evincing the sanctity of their professions by the innocence of their lives and the beneficence of their actions; for no man, who is profligate in his morals, or a bad member of the civil community, can possibly be a true Christian, or a credit to his own religious society."[146]

George Washington could be trusted with power. He recognized himself and others simply as unworthy servants of the great God of Abraham. He believed that adherence to the ways of Kind Providence brings blessings of peace and prosperity, which must be earned. He wrote:

"The man must be bad indeed who can look upon the events of the American Revolution without feeling the warmest gratitude towards the great Author of the Universe whose divine interposition was so frequently manifested on our behalf. And it is my earnest prayer that we may so conduct ourselves as to merit a continuance of those blessings with which we have hitherto been favored."[147]

At the Battle of Princeton, as was his custom during the Revolutionary War, Washington:

"[p]referred to risk his own life to achieve success rather than to remain safely behind his men and perhaps in consequence to receive reports of defeat. Conspicuous on a white horse, he rode forward within thirty yards of the British line, urging the men to follow him in attack. The smoke of gunfire enveloped him. His men feared that he was slain, but he was unscathed. The Patriots rallied behind him."[148]

Washington later said that his triumphs at Trenton and Princeton proceeded from good fortune. He knew that fortune favors the brave and the bold.[149] He also knew, adored and obeyed the Divine Source of good fortune. When his troops were weak from lack of food at Valley Forge, barefooted and persecuted by the bitter cold, art history records that their Commander-in-Chief faced that hardship on his knees in the snow. Such is the hero tradition he bequeaths.

History presents much to ponder about the benevolent hand of Divine Providence evident in Washington's life, victories and writings. Consider the following:

"His [Washington's] physical appearance was complemented by an aura, not merely of strength, but of invincibility. His immunity to gunfire seemed almost supernatural. Early in his career a treacherous guide fired at him from point-blank range-and missed. Once he rode between two columns of his own men who were firing at one another by mistake and struck up their guns with his sword.—the musket balls whizzed harmlessly by his head. Time and time again during the Revolutionary War musket balls tore his clothes, knocked off his hat, and shredded his cape; horses were killed under him; but he was never touched. What mortal could refuse to entrust his life to a man whom God obviously favored? What country could refuse to do so?"[150]

Washington's victories and accomplishments are models for all aspiring leaders, from small school children to exploring astronauts. Washington's expressed faith in the power of God's love to spawn human freedom is a luminescent torch of hope for seeking people. Washington's courage was horrifically assailed in battle, yet he never wavered. At the political formation of the government of the United States, his prayerful leadership, wielded for the most part in silent observance, engendered courageous vision among his colleagues. His steadfast humility throughout two terms as first President of a unique infant nation breathed life into government for the people, by the people and of the people. Washington consistently led by deeds and rarely by spoken word. His sacrificial, sagacious, largely hidden service in retirement shored up a fledgling nation struggling to become the domain of Kind Providence.

Today, in contemporary light, Washington's supernatural faith in action illumines the astonishing financial, political and diplomatic achievements of the American form of government. Washington's principled leadership flowed from his spiritual strength. His powerful integrity charted the course for America's soul-wrenching journey into the morning light of responsible freedom for God-fearing citizens.

PART THREE

Freedom's Triumph

General Washington recognized he would bear responsibility for America's victory or defeat.

CHAPTER SEVEN

In Defense of Freedom

*"...I shall never suffer private convenience to interfere
with what I conceive to be my official duties."*[151]
—*George Washington*

*I*n 1774, George Washington, representing Virginia, was a
member of the Continental Congress that assembled at
Philadelphia in the month of September. Unfortunately, a
self-appointed vigilante committee, The Association, hop-
ing to avoid separation from England had commissioned
themselves to oversee the daily activities of Americans
under the guise of 'encouraging frugality, economy and
industry, ...discontinuance of every species of extravagance
and dissipation, especially all horse-racing, and all kinds of
gaming, cock-fighting, exhibitions of shews, plays and other
expensive diversions and entertainments.' Though ill
advised members of the committee hoped The Association
would bring speedy concessions from the British Parliament,
it did not. A somewhat lawless state of affairs exacerbated a
fire keg mentality among the colonists. The Continental
Congress responded by drafting a Declaration of Rights and

Grievances, along with a plenary petition to the King of England. The Continental Congress ended but not before misunderstandings between the British monarchy and the colonists exploded.

The Revolutionary War began on the night of April 18, 1775, at Lexington, Massachusetts. Colonists quickly circulated the news that the King's forces had maliciously and wantonly opened fire, killing innocent, peaceful villagers. Of course, the story is not that simple. Nevertheless, eight Minutemen, as the patriot warriors were called, lay dead in the village square in the early morning light. On marched the British forces to Concord where the 'shot that was heard round the world' was fired. Then the British marched to Boston, but not before the death or maiming of 247 British Redcoats.

The second Continental Congress assembled in Philadelphia shortly thereafter on May 10, and a highly distinguished group it was. Though hopeful for conciliation with Great Britain, the mood of the men present was ominous. Each believed his cause was just, the Union a necessity. No one doubted God's will for the preservation of their liberties, being with one mind resolved to die free men rather than live as slaves to the whims of the British crown.[152]

By 23 June, 1776, it became clear that war with England was inevitable. George Washington, the most esteemed military leader among the Founders was appointed Commander-in-Chief of the American forces. He did not desire the post. His patriotism and high moral sense of stewardship however, left him no choice but to serve. He was quite obviously aware of the danger he was undertaking.

One of his first acts after the appointment was to draft a new Last Will and Testament, so as to provide for his wife, stepchildren, staff, employees, workers and slaves. He refused a salary for his services but asked the Congress to cover his expenses.[153] As the new Commander-in-Chief departed Philadelphia, a messenger met him along the road, bringing devastating news of the Battle of Bunker Hill.

Riding into battle with an ill-equipped, poorly trained militia comprised, among others, of farmers, fishermen and merchants, General Washington was aware that much of the world of his times lived in spiritual darkness.[154] His personal vision was guided by his commitment to live in Christian Light, to the best of his abilities.[155] This Virginia gentleman of the wilderness turned warrior knew His Creator deep in his soul.[156] He sincerely believed the American cause was just.[157] He simply and sincerely desired to be a faithful follower of Jesus Christ and serve God and the new nation.[158] His mottos were "Deeds, not words" and "For God and my Country."[159]

General Washington recognized he would bear personal responsibility for America's victory or defeat. He wrote:

> "...[F]ar from seeking this appointment (as Commander-in-Chief), I have used every endeavor in my power to avoid it....from the consciousness of its being a trust too great for my capacity.[160]

Washington addressed the horror of Bunker Hill with hope that Americans would achieve freedom to fully adhere to the natural law written upon their hearts without

governmental interference. Battle seemed the only alterna-
tive in those days and Washington fully resigned himself to
the call of duty. He and his troops would henceforth be
required to deliver the colonists from tyrannical oppressors
on their shores. Warrior that his fate called him to be,
Washington would pray and work and die for all law abiding
citizens to live freely in their new nation while actively pursuing happiness and prosperity.

By winter of 1777, Washington's courage and bravery
were sorely tested. His soldiers were ragged. They were hungry—even starving. They had nothing to keep them warm
that bitter winter except the fire of love in their hearts for
their families and the infant nation they struggled to cherish. These brave visionaries faced inhuman odds as the battle of Valley Forge loomed on the horizon.[161] Art history
reveals their commander-in-chief, in full view of his troops,
kneeling in the snow to implore the blessings and providence of Almighty God on the dedicated men who carried
the hopes and dreams of freedom in their hearts.

More things are wrought by prayer than this world fath-
oms. During those dark days of starvation and defeat at
Valley Forge, an extraordinary spiritual event may have
occurred sometime between the 18th and 23rd of
December.[162] Oral history and surviving historical data disclose a mysterious, unidentified, Beautiful Lady from
Heaven who appeared to console, inspire and guide the
needy General Washington.[163] One can only hypothesize
who that being of celestial splendor might have been.[164]
Some say it was the Guardian Angel of the United States.[165]

Historical precedent indicates the Beautiful Lady from Heaven may well have been Mary, the Mother of Jesus Christ, the Biblical Woman of Genesis (3:15). An explanation for that possibility rests in Washington's spiritual beliefs rooted in Anglican Catholicism. The Mother of Jesus Christ is and has always been deeply revered in the Anglican faith. No God-fearing Anglican would do less than to graciously honor the Mother of the Savior. Roman Catholics and Orthodox also honor Mary as Mother of God. Muslims honor the Blessed Virgin Mary only as Mother of Jesus.

General Washington, Christian that he was, as such would have believed that Jesus Christ is God Incarnate, a belief passed down from the Apostles. Mary supernaturally gave birth to the Savior who has taken on human flesh and blood and who, on the human level, comes from the same substance as His mother and all of us. At the same time, Jesus Christ is on the divine, consubstantial level of God the Father, Creator of all that is seen and unseen. Christianity holds that Jesus' substance is that of the Father.[166] Such belief would have been George Washington's faith. It would not have surprised a person of George Washington's background to encounter Mary in the depths of his anguish. John Marshall served with General Washington in the Revolutionary War, was first Secretary of State and first Chief Justice of the United States Supreme Court. He would have known George Washington well. He said of him: "Without making ostentatious professions of religion, he [George Washington] was a sincere believer in the Christian faith, and a truly devout man."

George Washington was an astute leader who consistently sought advice about matters outside his own frame of reference. Washington's business partner and confidante, Daniel Carroll was an educated Roman Catholic[167] whose younger brother, Jesuit John Carroll, studied for the priesthood in Liege, France. After enduring severe religious persecution, John returned to Maryland in 1774. He would have been an expert about Marian apparitions by seminary training and probably was aware of the mystical phenomenon General Washington experienced at Valley Forge.[168] Since George Washington was mostly silent about his personal spiritual experiences, his associates possibly learned about the Beautiful Lady from Heaven at Valley Forge from Archbishop Carroll, who would have recognized Mary's apparition to Washington as consistent with his faith tradition. On June 11, 1799, six months before General Washington's death, John Carroll conferred and dined with Washington at Mount Vernon. When he founded Georgetown University, George Washington was present.[169]

President Washington and Archbishop Carroll would have been keenly interested in the title "Son of the Republic" by which the Celestial Lady prophetically addressed George Washington at Valley Forge. It is probably not a coincidence that in his official capacity as First Archbishop of the United States, John Carroll, in 1792, solemnly and permanently entrusted the new nation and its citizens to the Blessed Mother Mary. President Washington, by now truly the "Son of the Republic," would of course have known of this sacred consecration and may have participated personally.

The text of the official consecration of the United States to Mary follows.

Consecration of the United States of America
to Mary

Most Holy Trinity, Our Father in Heaven,
Who chose Mary as the fairest of Your daughters;
Holy Spirit Who chose Mary as Your Spouse;
God the Son Who chose Mary as Your Mother,
In union with Mary, we adore Your Majesty
And acknowledge Your supreme, eternal dominion and authority.

Most Holy Trinity, we place the United States of America
Into the hands of Mary Immaculate
In order that she may present the country to You.
Through her we wish to thank You for the great resources of this land
And for the freedom which has been its heritage.

Through the intercession of Mary, have mercy on the
Catholic Church in America.
Grant us peace.
Have mercy on our President
And on all the officers of our government.

Grant us a fruitful economy, born of justice and labor.
Protect the family life of the nation.
Guard the precious gift of many religious vocations.
Through the intercession of Mary Our Mother, have mercy on the sick, the tempted, sinners....on all who are in need.

Mary, Immaculate Virgin, Our Mother,
Patroness of our land, we praise and honor you
And give ourselves to you.
Protect us from every harm.
Pray for us, that acting always according to your will
And the will of your Divine Son,
We may live and die pleasing to God. Amen.[170]
—John Carroll, 1792

Though the official Consecration does not prove the Blessed Mother Mary's apparition to General Washington at Valley Forge, it does lend it credibility. There is sufficient historical precedent that it actually was the Blessed Mother whom General Washington saw that bleak day at Valley Forge.[171] Through Mary, "the Mosaic Law arrived at the threshold of its fulfillment, and God's promise to the world and covenant with Abraham was fulfilled: 'God promised Abraham the forefather that in his seed shall the nations be blessed.... And through [Mary] the promise comes to pass....'"[172]

George Washington, the Commander-in-Chief of the American cause, had great need of divine intervention on

"*Gaze not at the marks or blemishes of others, and ask not how they came.
What you may speak in secret to your friend, deliver not before others.*"

8   *"Then their faith-filled Commander in Chief, in full view of his troops, knelt in the snow
to implore the blessings and providence of Almighty God on the dedicated men
who carried the hopes and dreams of freedom in their hearts."*

behalf of his highly distressed troops at Valley Forge. God has historically sent the Blessed Mother as ambassador of Divine Mercy, Comfort of the Afflicted in times of great human need.[173]

An eyewitness of George Washington's testimony of his celestial vision, Anthony Sherman later recounted segments of the heavenly phenomenon to Wesley Bradshaw. The oral history of this apparition to the American Commander-in-Chief at Valley Forge was published in *The National Tribune*, Volume 4, No. 12, December 1880, and is preserved in the Library of Congress in Washington, DC.[174]

"...From the opening of the (American) Revolution we experienced all phases of fortune, now good and now ill, one time victorious and another time conquered. The darkest period we had, I think, was when Washington, after several reverses, retreated to Valley Forge, where he resolved to pass the winter of 1777. Ah! I have often seen the tears course down our dear commander's careworn cheeks, as he would be conversing with confidential officers about the condition of his poor soldiers. You have doubtless heard the story of Washington going to the thicket to pray. It was not only true but he used often to pray in secret for aid and comfort from God, the Interposition of whose Divine Providence brought us safely through the darkest days of tribulation.

"One day, I remember it well, the chilly wind whistled through the leafless trees, though the sky was cloudless and the sun shone brightly. He remained in his quarters nearly all afternoon alone. When he came out I noticed that his face was a shade paler than usual, and there seemed to be something on his mind of more than ordinary importance. Returning just after dark, he dispatched an orderly to the quarters of another officer, who was presently in attendance. After a preliminary conversation of about half an hour, Washington, gazing upon us with that strange look of dignity, which he alone could command, said:

'I do not know whether it is owing to the anxiety of my mind, but this afternoon, as I was sitting at this table engaged in preparing a dispatch, something disturbed me. Looking up, I saw standing opposite a singularly beautiful female. So astonished was I, for I had given strict orders not to be disturbed, that it was some moments before I found language to inquire the purpose of her presence. A second, third, even a fourth time did I repeat my question but received no answer from my mysterious visitor, except a slight raising of her eyes. By this time I felt strange sensations spreading through me. I would have risen but the riveted gaze of the being before me rendered volition impossible. I essayed once more to address her, but my tongue had become useless. Even thought itself had become paralyzed. A new influence, mysterious, potent, irresistible, took possession of me. All I could do was to gaze steadily, at my unknown visitor. Gradually the surrounding atmosphere filled with sensation and grew luminous. Everything about me seemed to rarefy, the mysterious visitor herself becoming more airy and yet more distinct to my sight than before. I now began to feel as one dying, or rather to experience the sensation which I have sometimes imagined accompanies dissolution. I did not think, I did not reason, I did not move. All, alike, were impossible. I was conscious only of gazing fixedly at my companion.

'Presently I heard a voice say, **"Son of the Republic, look and learn!"** while at the same time my visitor extended her arm eastward. I looked and beheld a heavy white vapor rising, at some distance, fold upon fold. This gradually dissipated and I watched before me lay spread out in one vast plain all the countries of the world: Europe, Asia, Africa and America. I saw rolling and tossing between Europe and America, the billows of the Atlantic Ocean, and between America and Asia lay the Pacific.

"'Son of the Republic" said the mysterious voice as before, **"look and learn."** "At that moment I beheld a dark shadowy being, standing, or rather floating in mid-air between Europe and America. Dipping water out of the ocean with his right hand, he cast it upon America, while that in his left hand went upon the European countries. Immediately a cloud arose from these countries, and joined in mid-ocean. For awhile it remained stationery, and then it moved slowly westward, until it enveloped America in its folds. Sharp flashes of lighting gleamed through at intervals; and I heard the smothered groans of the American people. A second time the angel dipped water from the ocean and sprinkled it as before. The dark cloud was then drawn back to the ocean, in whose heaving bellows it sank from view.

'A third time I heard the mysterious voice say: **"Son of the Republic, look and learn."** "I cast my eyes upon America and beheld villages, towns and cities springing up one after another until the whole land, from the Atlantic to the Pacific, was dotted with them.

'Again I heard the voice say, **"Son of the Republic, the end of the century comes. Look and learn."** And with this the dark, shadowy angel turned its face southward, and from Africa an ill-omened spectra approached our land. It flitted slowly over every town and city of the land. The inhabitants presently set themselves in battle array against each other.

'As I continued to look I saw a bright angel, on whose brow rested a crown of light on which was traced the word UNION, place an American flag between the divided nation and say: **"Remember ye are brethren."** Instantly the inhabitants, casting from them weapons, became friends once more and united around the National Standard.

'Again I heard the voice of my most beautiful and mysterious visitor say, **"Son of the Republic, look and learn.** At this, the dark, shadowy angel placed a trumpet to his mouth and blew three distinct blasts; and taking water from the ocean he sprinkled it upon Europe, Asia and Africa.

'Then my eyes beheld a fearful scene: from each of these countries arose thick black clouds that were soon joined into one. Throughout this mass there gleamed a bright Red Light, by which I saw hordes of armed men, who, moving with the cloud, marched by land and sailed by sea to America which country was enveloped in the volume of cloud.

'And I saw these vast armies devastate the whole country and burn the villages, towns and cities that I saw springing up. As my ears listened to the thundering of the canon, the clashing of the swords, and the shouts and cries of millions in mortal combat, I again heard the mysterious voice say: **"Son of the Republic, look and learn."**

'As the voice ceased, the bright angel, for the last time, dipped water from the ocean and sprinkled it upon America. Instantly the dark cloud rolled back, together with the armies it had brought, leaving the inhabitants of the land victorious. Once more I beheld villages, towns and cities springing up where I had seen them before; while the bright angel, planting the azure standard he had brought in the middle of them, cried in a loud voice, "While the stars remain and the heavens send down dew upon the earth, so long shall the Union last."

'And taking from her angelic brow the crown on which was blazoned the word UNION, she placed it upon the National Standard, while people kneeling down, said, "Amen."

'The scene instantly began to fade away, and I saw nothing but the rising, curling vapor I had first beheld. This also disappeared and I found myself once more gazing upon the mysterious beautiful visitor who said, **"Son of the Republic, what you have seen is thus: three great perils will come upon the**

Republic. The most fearful is the third, but the whole world united shall not prevail upon her. Let every child of the Republic learn to live for God, his land and the Union." With these words the beautiful visitor and the bright angel accompanying her disappeared from my sight.

"Such, my friend, were the very words I heard from Washington's own lips and America will do well to profit by them," concluded the narrator of this Oral History.

Modern political scientists observe various historical trends and possibilities in prophetic scenes General Washington observed. Perhaps the most challenging is the tribulation of the third vision. Committed faithfulness to daily duty promises hard earned blessings as long as Americans "stand united, learning to live for God, their land and the Union." The strength of the Republic during more than 200 years stands surety for prophesies in the reported apparition.

Following General Washington's spiritual experience at Valley Forge, whatever it was for there is no other known record surviving of his personal recollections of the event, the tide of victory for the United States mysteriously turned. Prussian military expert Baron Friedrich Von Steuben made a commitment to train the American militia at Valley Forge and the French decided to becomes allies of the new nation.

Victory for the United States was far from easy. Immense darkness enveloped the American cause by the early months of 1781. Washington was put to further spiritual tests as he endured his own "agony in the garden." Was this war and his role in it really the plan of Kind Providence for the Western Hemisphere? And if so, did he truly trust God's power, in spite of the obvious poverty and inadequacy of his troops?[175]

Washington had a pitiful army, even after the best efforts of General Von Steuben. The fact that the continental currency was often worthless allowed the States to refuse to honor requisitions for even the most basic needs of the Revolutionary Forces. A Pennsylvania regiment, overcome by the lack of clothing and food actually mutinied.

Washington prayed. No serious historian disputes General Washington's outspoken reliance on Kind Providence. Quite correctly, on a human level he realized that no victory would be possible without superior sea power. Washington wrote an urgent message to French General Rochambeau who had six thousand men sequestered at Newport, Rhode Island, pleading for quick and decisive help:

"In any operation, and under all circumstances, a decisive naval superiority is to be considered a fundamental principle, and the basis upon which every hope of success must ultimately depend."[176]

Simultaneously, Washington dispatched a special envoy to King Louis XVI in Paris with his pressing request for immediate naval assistance. Washington prevailed. Through the masterful diplomatic skills of Benjamin Franklin, France entered the American Revolution on the side of the colonists.

French naval help was quick, powerful and decisive. Admiral Compte de Grasse was dispatched to the rescue and sailed from Haiti on August 5, with his great fleet of four thousand men and a treasure chest filled with negotiable currency. On August 25, Admiral DeBarras' fleet, conveying Rochambeau's siege artillery, sailed from Newport, Rhode Island to the Chesapeake. The naval strategy was to overcome the British stronghold at the Chesapeake but DeBarras had to get past the English fleet harbored in New York. Kind Providence has dominion over all reality. Unexplained confusion surrounded Charles Cornwallis' British commanders who were entrenched in the New York harbors. A mysterious fog enshrouded the harbor at the Battle of Brooklyn Hill. Perhaps miraculously, the English failed to grasp the significance of French naval strategies, unfolding in front of them in New York harbor as the fleet slipped past them.

By August 30, 1781, the French were now masters of the Chesapeake. On September 5, French officers who brought General Washington news of De Grasse's plenary tactics noted that they had never seen a man express so much joy. They wrote:

"The General 'acted like a child whose every wish [prayer] had been gratified.'"[177]

The British fleet departed the Virginia coast by September 14 and returned to New York. Washington and the allied armies under him, commanded by Rochambeau, Lafayette and Saint-Simon, along with 1500 of the ever faithful Virginia militia, besieged Cornwallis' stronghold at Yorktown, beginning on September 30. On October 17, 1781, the defeated Cornwallis surrendered.[178]

Thirteen United States Colonies sent Commissioners to Paris to negotiate peace with Great Britain. Throughout the long negotiations, Washington remained calm, humble and a voice of peace and reason in the United States. A definitive peace treaty was finally concluded on September 3, 1783.

CHAPTER EIGHT

America's Prosperity

"...I hope someday or another, we shall become a store-house and granary for the world."[179]
—George Washington

*H*istory has canonized George Washington as the most esteemed of the Founding Fathers for many reasons. Without his transfiguring faith, personal selfsacrifice, expertise and, most significantly of all, victory on the battlefield, the Declaration of Independence would have been a seal of defeat and certain death for the signers. Washington's amazingly modest, brilliant and severely tested leadership assured that the extraordinary "government of the people, by the people and for the people" did not crumble in the sands of humanity's unrealized dreams.

Washington, a refined Christian gentleman, muscular, powerful, with high cheek bones, piercing blue eyes, insightful intelligence, steady humor and consistent patience courageously carried America's dreams for freedom to fulfillment. He did not work alone. No one does. Humble

Washington surrounded himself with outstanding leaders of every region, faith and national background. He made it clear however, that he would always bow before Kind Providence, from Whom all blessings and prosperity flow. Those who would serve with him would necessarily do the same. Washington was not a theologian or a philosopher by nature. He was practical, with down to earth faith, coupled with political sensitivity. His leadership was rooted in the spiritual philosophy of the neophyte American system of private enterprise. Washington had an indomitable belief that every person is gifted and endowed with the possibility of help by Jesus Christ the Savior to live peacefully, seeking prosperity and pursuing happiness if he but follows the divine laws written upon his heart by his Creator, Kind Providence.

Washington was highly organized. He kept a daily journal in which he faithfully recorded where and how his time and money were spent. His records show that he was prayerful, disciplined and frugal by nature. However, he expended lavishly to enrich his family, home, employees, and slaves whom he treated as citizens of Mount Vernon at a time when Virginia accorded them no rights at all. His generosity to his Country and countrymen is unmatched. Washington believed that prayer, hard work and sacrificial discipline bring the Creator's reciprocal gift of wisdom, a constant companion of those who succeed in life.

Washington's colleagues in the pursuit of American private enterprise were a formidable team. Benjamin Franklin of Pennsylvania, John Adams of Massachusetts, Roger Sherman of Connecticut, Robert R. Livingston of New York and Thomas Jefferson of Virginia, men of varied spiritual beliefs, drafted the Declaration of Independence in 1776. They submitted it to the Continental Congress on the twenty-eighth of June in that year. On July 4, 1776, after vigorous debate, men representing the united colonies on the North American continent ratified the document, thereby declaring themselves and their constituents a free, independent nation in the world. By one signature, that of John Hancock, President of the Congress, the Declaration of Independence became a beacon of freedom for the entire world to see, and created a land of unparalleled prosperity. On August 2, 1776, 55 of the 56 signers also placed their signatures on the Declaration of Independence. Finally and before year-end, Matthew Thornton's signature completed the unanimous document that gave life to the United States of America.

The colonists believed the major role of government is to protect private property. Ninety percent were farmers, the typical farm being 90 to 160 acres. These farmers were self sufficient folk. Hired men, usually newer immigrants, indentured servants and slaves worked the farms. A typical white colonial family had the highest standard of living in the world. They were healthier and taller than Europeans, better educated, and thanks to Bibles and newspapers that proliferated throughout the colonies, they were the most literate, God-fearing people in the world. At that time, many rights were reserved for white men who owned a certain amount of property. Women, free white men who owned no property, free black men, slaves, Native Americans and indentured servants had no civil rights. They depended on the moral righteousness of the white men for their well-being. When the interference of the English monarchy became intolerable for everyone, revolution was inevitable.

The spirit of individual and financial freedom became a gale force in the colonies. A careful review of the language of the Declaration of Independence discloses contempt the founders held for unjust policies and corrupt authority. Americans were unwilling to accept self-appointed, unelected humans alleging divine rights to kill, exploit, pillage and loot private property. That courageous position, though brave, was as dangerous and costly then as it remains today.

With more than two thousand miles of ocean to separate them from European shores, the colonists had survived by growing in wisdom and renewed reverence for the laws and rewards of Almighty God. The Bible, available and widely read in the colonies, revealed the power of God's grace and inspired the hearts of God-fearing colonial men and women. Their heightened Biblical awareness of liberty under just law prevented them from bowing before tyranny from any source. The Sacred Word enjoined them to protect themselves from human predators, even at the cost of their own lives. The Declaration of Independence was written with the ink of spiritual revolution that would soon turn to human blood. Only faith in God's powerful, omniscient, all loving Providence and hope in a better, more egalitarian life for every man, woman and child could spur such patriotism.

Washington and his colleagues perceived a natural meritocracy among people, grounded in virtue and talents.[180] Idolatrous ancient aristocracy with its unearned privileges and wealth was not for America. George Washington and his peers lived their belief that the Creator breathes all people out of His Heart of love. Each comes into the world endowed with certain unalienable rights, among which are life, liberty and the pursuit of happiness. Embracing scriptural principles as a blueprint for human development, the Founders inspired people of the thirteen colonies to rise to the heights of fortitude and courage. Americans sought to earn the Biblical rewards of prosperity, long life, health, wisdom, peace steeped in the way, the truth and the light of God's revealed laws and promises.

The Founding Fathers, under Washington's leadership, drew deeply upon Judeo-Christian roots and concepts of duty among Colonists of every belief, race and nation. The seriousness of this commitment pervades the language of the Declaration of Independence and the Constitution with its Bill of Rights which followed in 1791. The Bible illumined the way to liberty and its rewards of prosperity and happiness in the new republic, one nation under God. All citizens were and are expected to ascend the heights of spiritual righteousness for their own good, the good of those with whom they live and the planet itself.

In the war against England, Washington and his coterie pledged their lives, their fortunes and their sacred honor as surety for the success of their cause.[181] Such sacrifice is the heart of the ancient Christian ethic centered in the cross of Jesus Christ. The signers of the Declaration of Independence included themselves in the first group called to die for the cause if captured. Their stated goal was to bring forth a new nation conceived in liberty and dedicated to the proposition that all people are in fact divinely created equal in dignity before God and one another. As such, each is entitled to life, liberty and the pursuit of happiness. With the stroke of their pen on that life-giving document, each signer became a notorious traitor, punishable by death under English law.

Recognizing that a brutal war lay on the horizon, for tyrants hold fast to their prey, General Washington rallied the colonists. These people were not warriors. They were simply farmers, fur traders, merchants and fishermen. His singular leadership passionately prepared peace-loving men to shed their last drop of blood rather than yield their property, their livelihood and their freedom. Tyranny and oppression from absentee rulers were incompatible with the winds of liberty that the colonists enjoyed. From the beginning, the underlying principles of the United States included the sacredness and inherent value of each unique human life and the inviolate right to own and enjoy private property.

By the time Washington was appointed commander-in-chief of the Revolutionary Forces, he was married to Martha Dandridge Custis, a wealthy widow with two small children. She was one of the richest women in Virginia.[182] Their life together at Mount Vernon was full and quite pleasing to the General. Mrs. Washington, though plump, was small in stature, five feet tall. She was not born to wealth but inherited it from her first husband. Those who knew her said she was modest and sweet tempered, not at all spoiled by her great wealth, which passed into George Washington's hands at their marriage. She was "…a lady in manners and in conduct about whom there was never a word of scandal."[183] Her biographer, Joseph E. Fields, writes of Martha Washington:

"In many ways, Martha Washington was the ideal woman for the new American republic. She was not born of the aristocracy, but she gained the admiration and respect of all classes of people. She was devoted to family and home, but she really made personal sacrifices to join her husband in his public duties. ...During the Presidency, she was called both dignified and democratic as she forged the role of the President's wife that would be followed for generations to come. She neither sought nor relished her public positions, but carried out the duties that were thrust upon her with enormous consideration and care. Her simple appearance bespoke quality rather than ostentation...."[184]

Abigail Adams, wife of John Adams wrote:

"Mrs. Washington is one of those unassuming characters which create Love and esteem." In her presence, Mrs. Adams admitted she found herself "much more deeply impressed than I ever did before their Majesties of Britain."[185]

The commander-in-chief loved his wife dearly. Martha's virtues certainly influenced Washington. Her calming presence and steadfastness in his life provided comfort, support and the joy of her two young children whom Washington raised as his own. Mrs. Washington, though she never bore a child for the General, was with him at Valley Forge, Boston, and other places of difficulty during the Revolutionary War. She cared for his beloved Mount Vernon during his long absences and entertained dignitaries, statesmen and ordinary citizens for him during his long career in government.

She carried out his wishes concerning the slaves of Mount Vernon, educating the children and emancipating them all.

Martha and George Washington's kindness and commitment to one another exemplified the ideals of the times in the United States where godliness implies an individual, God-given right to think, believe and respond to God's divine presence without coercion. They cherished their rights to own and protect private property without undue disturbance and to pursue personal happiness.

Washington, with his gentle Martha at his side, enjoyed many of life's pleasures. He drank fine tea, sipped excellent wine, danced at social events, played cards and billiards with gentlemen and shared his pleasing sense of humor. Though Washington encouraged learning, he never did so at the expense of duty to entrusted assets and obligations. He believed that education without faith was a waste. He bought his stepson books of theology, philosophy, arithmetic, science, history, English poetry and travel. He consistently encouraged his stepson to grow in consonance with his station in life as a Christian and a patriot. He also urged him to learn enlightened ways of farming the fertile Virginia land. Washington at heart believed as a farmer that he was a trustee of God's earth. A true environmentalist, he loved the earth's munificence. His great love for nature inspired him to become one of the most successful land speculators of his times.[186]

George and Martha Washington were generous stewards of God's goodness to them. Their joy was to share their blessings. One biographer, Lonnelle Aikman writes of a typical Christmas dinner at Mount Vernon:

"Christmas dinner with the Washington's at Mount Vernon brings on the usual good food and good conversation. Many guests who sat at this table wrote glowingly of both. One recalled an impressive menu of 'roasted pigg, boiled leg of lamb, roasted fowls, beef, peas, lettuce, cucumbers, artichokes, etc., puddings, tarts, etc., etc.' For drinks there was a choice of wines, beer, or cider. It was then the custom to serve dinner in mid-afternoon, tea at six, and supper, if desired, at about nine."[187]

Guided by their Christian faith, Washington and his wife were quite compatible and he was faithful to her.[188] Washington never engaged in duels though he was an able swordsman with developed fencing skills, nor resorted to violence with his peers or underlings. He was slow to anger, but fierce in battle when aroused.[189] Washington preferred the presence of polite ladies and gentlemen at Mount Vernon rather than rough, unpolished soldiers and frontiersmen.[190] He was distinguished for his courtesy. Biographer John R. Alden reported of Washington:

"He developed a cool and discriminating judgment and with it a remarkable ability to take advantage of the insights of other men."[191]

Washington was a temperate man who led by example. He forbade vulgarity, womanizing and profanity among his troops, employees and slaves. He expressed his views on the dangers of consuming intoxicating liquor to one of his over-seers.

"...[R]efrain from spirituous liquors; they will prove your ruin if you do not. Consider how little a drunk-en man differs from a beast; the latter is not endowed with reason, the former deprives himself of it; and when that is the case, acts like a brute, annoying and disturbing everyone around him. Nor is this all, nor as it respects himself, the worst of it. By degrees, it renders a person feeble, and not only unable to serve others but to help himself; and being an act of his own, he falls from a state of usefulness into contempt, and at length suffers, if not perishes in penury and want."[192]

George Washington as Founding Father claimed for himself, his loved ones and those he served individual, per-sonal freedom of thought, religious belief, political persua-sion, and a life grounded in the laws of God and of nature. In a public address at a great civic banquet in Philadelphia, on April 20, 1789, celebrating his unanimous election as First President of the United States, Washington said:

"When I contemplate the interposition of Providence, as it was manifested in guiding us through the Revolution, in preparing us for the reception of a general government, and in conciliat-ing the good will of the people of America towards one another after its adoption, I feel myself oppressed and almost overwhelmed with a sense of divine munificence. I feel that nothing is due to my personal agency in all these complicated and wonderful events, except what can simply be attributed to the exertions of an honest zeal for the good of my country.

"If I have distressing apprehensions, that I shall not be able to justify the too exalted expectations of my countrymen, I am supported under the pressure of such uneasy reflections by a confidence that the most gracious Being, who has hitherto watched over the interests and averted the perils of the United States, will never suffer so fair an inheritance to become a prey to anarchy, despotism, or any other species of oppression."[193]

To understand Washington's God as Kind Providence, and the source of American prosperity, one need only consider the number and variety of active, thriving churches, temples, synagogues, mosques, sports arenas, schools, universities and businesses per capita in the United States. The faith of George Washington, Founding Father, lives in the accomplishments of American youth, in the output of American industry, in technological, diplomatic, military, social and medical advances that break global curses of isolation, ignorance, poverty, sickness and war. American prosperity is rooted in the glorious diversity and spiritual depth of its varied people.

The presence and cultural heritage of Native Americans added dignity and grace to the emerging United States. Indians, as Columbus mistakenly named them, welcomed Europeans as "men from heaven."[194] They taught the newcomers how to farm, fish, hunt and survive in North America. Medicine men, citing the ways of the "Great Spirit," provided drug remedies that were sought after by the more enlightened because of their heightened effectiveness against disease.

Either knowingly or through the aegis of Kind Providence, early Americans embraced Godly virtues. They created a governmental framework in which individual expression of love and commitment, labor and thrift are rewarded with prosperity. Reflecting his own vision of prosperous stewardship, Washington was an honest and shrewd businessman.[195] His business education was rooted in the Bible. In the book of Genesis, the Bible recounts God's plan for managing financial resources. Beginning with revelations to Abraham, father in faith of Hebrews, Christians and Muslims, God offers rewards and punishments that affect human wealth, health and happiness.

When Abraham was seventy-five years old, he heard the voice of the Lord commanding him: "Go forth from the land of your kinfolk and from your father's house to the land that I will show you."[196] This was a difficult order, yet one that God would issue time and again throughout ensuing centuries to countless others. God told Abraham to leave everyone and everything he knew and loved except for his half sister Sarah, daughter of his father but not of his mother, whom he had taken as his wife. She was quite beautiful. Things went well for Abraham wherever he wandered.

The Nomadic Abraham arrived in Egypt without money and perhaps afraid. Because Sarah was so enticing, the Pharaoh took her for his wife, believing that she was merely Abraham's sister. But God does not tolerate adultery for long. Pharaoh's house was struck with severe plagues. When the afflicted Pharaoh realized the source of his suffering, he commanded that Abraham take back Sarah, along with restitution of herds and flocks, male and female slaves, asses and camels. Only then did the plagues abate in the Pharaoh's personal household and throughout his kingdom.

Abraham and Sarah were now rich in livestock, silver and gold. They were financially rewarded for Abraham's obedience to the voice of God which sent him and Sarah forth into distant, unfamiliar, mysterious places with nothing but faith in God's providence as their guiding light. Abraham and Sarah continued their travels in obedience to the Lord's voice which guided Abraham.

Now steward of vast resources and assets, Abraham not only had responsibility for Sarah, but he also was called to actively manage diverse people, flocks and herds of animals. Abraham, investing multiple currencies, became in effect an international banker and diplomat, negotiating, trading and engaging in guerrilla wars along the way. Hearing the Lord, he became expert at leveraging and bartering his passage across the desert in obedience to the calls of the Lord.

George Washington would have been a student of Abraham's relationship with God. He, like Abraham, invoked the Lord by name in prayer. The more adroit Abraham became at listening to the Lord, discerning God's will and obeying, the more successful he became in his accomplishments. So also it was with George Washington. Abraham learned that no encounter on the earth is a coincidence. Opportunity for improvement of people, places and things lies hidden in every meeting. Washington too, a faithful son of Abraham, lived by that truth.

Delegates to the Constitutional Convention under the able leadership of George Washington "crafted a secular state, one that dared not establish, support, and defend religion. Indeed, the end result of the Founding Fathers' deliberations was the acknowledgement that religion is not, nor should it ever be under government jurisdiction, remaining one of those natural rights that the people retain for themselves."[197]

The framers of the Constitution created a document that made the United States the most religiously free nation state in the world. The Constitution of the United States guarantees that personal religion and political power binding people under one form of government are entirely separate. The United States, by law and precedent, has a free religious market; never governmental coercion. Every citizen carries the natural right to worship God as his or her conscience dictates.

Washington's spiritual leadership in the free market place of commerce and ideas casts a long shadow. In the early days of John Adam's presidency, a Treaty of Peace and Friendship between the United States and Tripoli was negotiated by the executive branch of the U.S. government and

presented to the Senate, which after due deliberation ratified the Treaty. Of great interest to New England merchants
and investors, this treaty with the Muslim power carved out
shipping protection for American ships in Barbary trading
waters. Article 11 of the Treaty contained significant language   guaranteeing   religious   freedom   under   the
Constitution of the United States.

> "As the government of the United States of America
> is not in any sense founded on the Christian
> Religion,—as it has in itself no character of enmity
> against the laws, religion, or tranquility of
> Musselmen,—and as the said States never have
> entered into any war or act of hostility against any
> Mehomitan nation, it is declared by the parties that
> no pretext arising from religious opinions ever pro-
> duce an interruption of the harmony existing
> between two countries."[198]

Americans deeply imbibe the elixir of religious freedom
won in the early days of the Republic. It is widely understood
that no secular power has the authority to govern religion for
it is a wholly private, individual right.

George Washington, the spiritual man was sacrificial
and generous with his time, talents and assets. Kind
Providence rewarded him accordingly. During his lifetime,
God graciously endowed him with the gift of wisdom with
which, among other things, he increased rather than dissipated his wealth. Though he had only a life interest in
Mount Vernon, he was able to acquire seven thousand acres

adjacent to his Potomac Riverfront property. He wisely enjoyed prosperity enough to share it generously. More than two hundred years later, much of the world seeks the ways of freedom and abundance that George Washington found in his lifetime.

CHAPTER NINE

Washington's Legacy

"Integrity and firmness is all I can promise; these, be the voyage long or short, never shall forsake me although I may be deserted by all men."[199]—*George Washington*

*G*eneral Washington's influence was extensive. Nevertheless, he resigned his commission at Annapolis in 1783 and retired to his beloved Mount Vernon. His advice was widely sought in the formation of the new national and state governments. Washington, who wrote at least 4,000 letters in his lifetime, duly noted his recollection of the business of his life of service years later in 1797:

> "...[U]nless someone pops in unexpectedly, Mrs. Washington and I will do what has not been (done) by us in nearly 20 years—that is sit down to dinner by ourselves.[200]

The spirituality of the times which Washington so faithfully embraced and exemplified is discernible in the humanitarian nature of the disciplines undertaken in the newly developing United States. There was widespread conviction that the gentleman of pleasure was a plague to himself as well as to his society, and particularly in times of crisis.[201] Consequently, inventions proliferated and nature's secrets were investigated assiduously. Literature and the arts flourished. Business and commerce thrived. It was understood that the vices and foibles of society derive fundamentally from a lack of work discipline and the virtuous habits which the maintaining of good fortune require.[202]

Godly men of destiny met in the State House at Philadelphia beginning in May of 1787 to draft a Federal Constitution for the United States. Dutiful Washington once again left his home at Mount Vernon to serve his country as a representative from Virginia. Under his watchful, though mostly silent leadership, the Federal Convention created a framework for the United States government that endures to this day. Dickinson, a Pennsylvanian, announced a clear break with the intellectuals of the "Age of Reason" thereby setting the tone for the document with the words: "Experience must be our only guide. Reason may mislead us." The most tested, experienced leader present was George Washington.

Embracing the freedom of their newly ratified Constitution, the people of the United States elected their first President, a hero whose tested leadership was totally steeped in commitment to God's ways. Washington was their unanimous choice. His new job was Herculean. Documents, dreams and realities of the new-born United States of America sprang to life in the nurturing light of George Washington's trustful, faith-filled spirituality.

Many appreciate the depth of Washington's religious conviction that "…God would hold him accountable for the ultimate meaning of American independence as revealed by history."[203] Disobedience to God's ways, as they understood them, continued to be the cardinal transgression of the times. Racial heterogeneity and social structure ranged from sophisticated, rich East Coast merchants to rebellious frontiersmen. Such diversity was obviously God's plan for the new nation from the beginning.

George Washington was so beloved by the populace that he could have allowed himself to become King of America. Many in fact desired to crown him. Such adulation was not attractive to the first President of the United States. After having served two full terms in office, in retirement he chose to remain an ordinary citizen and return to his family duties at Mount Vernon. Power did not corrupt this leader for he was a highly tested bearer of wisdom and humility.

The final years of Washington's life passed peacefully and productively at his beloved Mount Vernon, along the shores of the Potomac River. An analysis of his home life, management of his plantation and writings disclose hints of Washington's deep spiritual detachment from all that is not of God, for God, with God, and in God. George Washington acquired that spiritual freedom during a lifetime of service to his family, community and nation that required him to ascend the mountains of asceticism.

By 1799, Washington spoke frequently and in quite a matter of fact manner of the limited days that remained to him on earth. He was keenly aware that he was approaching the Biblical three score and ten.

> "He worked strenuously to organize his affairs, all for which he was responsible in such a manner so as to bring no burden upon anyone… 'that no reproach may attach itself to me when I have taken my departure for the land of the spirits.'"[204]

After his youngest brother died in the summer of 1799, Washington lamented: "I am the first, and am now the last of my father's children by the second marriage who remain. When I shall be called upon to follow them is known only to the Giver of life."[205]

Martha Washington was aware of her spouse's premonition of impending death. She wrote the following letter to a relative on September 18, 1799.

> "At midsummer the General had a dream so deeply impressed on his mind that he could not shake it for several days. He dreamed that he and I were sitting in the summer-house, conversing about the happy life we had spent, and looking forward to many more years on the earth, when suddenly there was a great light all around us, and then an almost invisible figure of a sweet angel stood by my side and whispered in my ear. I suddenly turned pale and then began to vanish from his sight and he was left alone. I had just

risen from the bed when he awoke and told me his dream, saying, 'You know a contrary result indicated by dreams may be expected. I may soon leave you.' I tried to drive from his mind the sadness that had taken possession of it, by laughing at the absurdity of being disturbed by an idle dream, which, at the worst, indicated that I would not be taken from him; but I could not, and it was not until after dinner that he recovered any cheerfulness. I found in the library, a few days afterwards, some scraps of paper which showed that he had been making a Will, and had copied it…"[206]

Historical records reveal Washington on December 9, five days before his death. His nephew recounted:

"It was a bright frosty morning; he had taken his usual ride and the clear health flush on his cheek and his sprightly manner brought the remark from both of us that we had never seen the General look so well. I have sometimes thought him decidedly the handsomest man I ever saw; and when in a lively mood, so full of pleasantry, so agreeable to all with whom he associated that I could hardly realize that he was the same Washington whose dignity awed all who approached him."[207]

The date was December 12 and Washington mounted his huge white horse by ten o'clock. The master of Mount Vernon's hair, by now no longer prematurely gray as it had been after the war, was totally white. And soon the weather at Mount Vernon turned from drizzling rain to white snow flakes. His thoughts are unknown. Christmas was 13 days away.

His pious wife Martha, true to her spiritual duties, may have been sitting by the fire in the parlor with her Bible and Anglican Book of Common Prayer, deeply engrossed in her daily commitment to one hour every morning for devotions.[208] Perhaps Washington had his "...beautifully printed Book of Psalms"[209] in his coat pocket. Washington probably knew the contents by heart. Before the War of Independence, the General had purchased this prayer book from London and the record discloses that he knew the contents of the book well. "...many of its descriptions of the Creator and Divine Architect seeped into his written imagery. The psalms of David describe a God who acts in history. Washington and his men publicly prayed that God would act on their behalf... as he had done on behalf of the first Israel."[210]

Washington's ride that day included his entire estate at Mount Vernon. He certainly saw the homes of three hundred slaves. Only a third of the slave population was able to engage in productive work. The rest depended upon the General and his wife to care for them. Doggedly, at great personal sacrifice, and contrary to the culture and mores of his time, and the laws of Virginia, Washington refused to sell or disperse slave families. Fatherly as he was, George Washington forbade separation of slave families. His slaves, legally his personal property, were intermarried with Martha's slaves over whom he had no direct authority. They belonged to the Custis Estate. If Washington had emancipated his own slaves, it would have disrupted the slaves' family lives, sending them far away while their family members necessarily remained behind. At that time, slaves had no rights or protection under the laws of Virginia. Their entire well-being depended on their owner's decisions.

At Mount Vernon, George and Martha Washington provided the equivalent of village life for their slave population fairly, yet generously, both in difficult and comfortable economic times. In April of 1786, he wrote to Robert Morris:

"I can only say that there is not a man living who wishes more sincerely than I do, to see a plan adopted for the abolition of it [slavery]—but there is only one proper and effectual mode by which it can be accomplished, & that is by Legislative authority: and this, as far as my suffrage will go, shall never be wanting."[211]

General Washington wrote of his dilemma concerning his slaves to his nephew Robert Lewis.

"To sell the overplus [unneeded slaves] I cannot because I am prejudiced against this kind of traffic in human species; to hire them out is almost as bad, because they cannot be disposed of in families to any advantage, and to divide families, I have an aversion."[212]

Washington, a just and moral man, understood that slavery of any kind is unjust and immoral.[213] He was the only Founding Father to free his slaves. By his final Will and Testament, he decreed that all Mount Vernon slaves be freed upon the death of his wife. By his providential reversionary interest in Mount Vernon, he retained legal rights to accomplish that emancipation, but only after his death and the death of his wife. Washington directed his Executors to provide for the aged blacks out of the assets of his estate, which required payments for their well being until the death of the last survivor in 1833. Washington further provided that, before emancipation of the slave children, they be taught to read and write and brought to some useful occupation, even though the laws of Virginia forbade the education of slaves.[214] Martha carried out her husband's wishes. Within a year of his death, slave children who had been taught to read and write were among the plantation's 300 emancipated slaves.

George Washington, perhaps the wisest man of his times, was among the most traveled of men in the United States. Combat, and later his presidency, had taken him to all the States. Former slaves, as free men, fought side by side in the North with white colonists in the Revolutionary War under his command. Washington respected American slaves as children of God and truly desired to see them emancipated. Yet he knew he lived in a historical lag and that only a strong federal government could make emancipation a reality. As a visionary, he could hope for more enlightened times and a leader like Abraham Lincoln. As a General, he could mourn the blood soaked price emancipation would exact.

George Washington was a tested man who appreciated the power, beauty, bounty and cruelty of nature. Perhaps he saw in the wonders of nature a tiny hint of God's presence. Washington, with his much loved staff, worked tirelessly to beautify Mount Vernon, to make it bountiful and prosperous for all. Here was a man called to heal and restore creation, not just for himself, and the few who surrounded him, but for all.

Washington had valuable gifts of the spirit. Wisdom was in his heart. Knowledge pleased his soul. Discretion watched over him. Understanding guarded him. Rectitude and justice were his aides de camp. Honesty lighted his path. These gifts were safe with humble George Washington and available for the good of humanity because he allowed himself to be guided by the kindness of God Almighty. Nothing displays his kinship with the great God of Abraham more profoundly than the circumstances of his death.

Washington's deathbed suffering was accepted lovingly by America's Founding Father as a gentle gift flowing from Kind Providence. He realized that anything short of perfect abandonment to the ways of Kind Providence would be the ultimate defilement of his immortal soul and consummate defeat. By this time in his life, Washington had fought the good fight. Any deep-seated behavior reflecting insensitivity to sin was mollified by the time the Founding Father succumbed to death's call.

Washington's secretary and executive assistant, Tobias Lear, recorded some of the circumstances surrounding his last hours.[215] But there may be personal information Lear chose to withhold or alter for national or international diplomatic reasons. Lear was a deist. He was responsible for public announcements regarding the most famous man in the world. Who really knows what influence he exerted in selectively sorting George Washington's written record, or even fabricating or altering, with the best of intentions, George Washington's personal handwritten record? "During his fourteen years with Washington, he had learned to reproduce not only Washington's handwriting, but also his written and spoken style."[216]

It is known for sure that Washington's final and greatest battle began that dreary December day in 1799. Washington rode on despite the inclement weather for he had work to do on the plantation. He knew well that faith must have works to express itself, personally and in the service of others. Many depended on Washington for their daily bread. He chose, with Herculean effort, to bring to perfection his earthly activities "works." Washington the planter knew rain and snow water God's earth with new life. Driving rain and new snow did not deter the General from his daily duties.

An abrupt change in the weather changed the snow to sleet that day. During Washington's five-hour ride around the plantation, the sleet changed into cold, steady rain that turned again to snow. When he came into the house at 3 o'clock, his face was ruddy, the back of his neck covered with fresh snow matching his white hair. But he said he felt quite well. Washington ate his meal that evening and those who were with him found him to be as hearty and thoughtful as usual.

The next day, on December 13, the plantation was covered with snow. Washington, experiencing a sore throat, stayed in doors for most of the day. When the snow stopped at four o'clock, the General went outside to the front lawn to mark specific trees to be removed. George and Martha sat by the fire in the parlor after they finished their evening meal. Though his voice was hoarse, Washington read aloud from gazettes for her edification. When it was suggested that he take something for his cold, Washington said he never took anything for a cold. Rather, he preferred to "let it go as it came."[217]

George and Martha retired at their usual time. They shared a double bed with a white canopy and white hanging curtains around the mahogany headboard. A roaring fire in the fireplace made the room cozy in spite of the howling wind and driving snow. During the night, in the early hours of December 14, Washington experienced severe chills and fever. His great difficulty in breathing awakened his wife sometime between 2 and 3 AM. She saw that he was in much distress and could hardly speak. Though Martha desired to summon a servant for help, Washington restrained her fearing for her health in the cold room. He endured his difficulties silently, lovingly encouraging Martha to go back to sleep. Finally a morning servant arrived to lay the fire at 7 AM. Martha then quickly summoned help for the ailing General.

By now he could not swallow, and his words were becoming somewhat unintelligible. During the next thirteen hours, he was bled four times. Of course, the procedure, standard in the medical community at the time, served only to weaken him further. Washington mentioned about his throat: "Tis very sore." Other than that, no complaints were heard at all. He had either a severe streptococcus infection,[218] or "…most probably suffered from a virulent bacterial infection of the epiglottis."[219]

Washington insisted upon getting dressed that day. After sitting by the fire in his bedroom for about two hours without relief, he returned to his bed. By 4:30, Washington quietly said to the doctor in attendance: "Doctor, I die hard. But I am not afraid to go."[220] Washington was suffering immensely. Finally, he said "I feel myself going. I thank you for your attention. You had better not take any more trouble about me; but let me go off quietly; I cannot last long."[221] He asked for Martha to join him. His courage allowed her and others gathered around him to see that suffering is a gift and a test of a soul's capacity to love.[222]

He who had escaped death so many times on the battlefield knew well there is a time to die. No one disputes the brilliant faith of George Washington. It is widely circulated that Washington, or perhaps those around him sent for his Minister to join him in his preparations to meet his Maker. Such a private religious act, of course would not be promulgated to the public. The Minister was no where to be found on such short notice. In the mysterious aegis of Divine Providence, the only clergyman available, so the oral history that circulates to this day holds, was Reverend Francis Neale, a Jesuit priest from the Society of Jesus in Maryland Province. George Washington, forever the man of destiny is said to have accepted his fate peacefully. The immortal Founding Father of the United States, great grandson of a persecuted Anglican Catholic priest, so some say, humbly confessed his sins, received the Blessed Sacrament, and final anointing with Holy Oil."[223]

During the last hours of Washington's life, three medical providers are recorded by Tobias Lear as having been in attendance. His lifelong friend, Dr. Craik, Dr. Elisha Cullen Dick of Alexandria and Dr. Gustavus Richard Brown of Port Tobacco conferred about the ailing General's condition:

> "Drs Craik and Brown agreed on the diagnosis of quinsy (an extreme form of tonsillitis) and urged further debilitating treatment—more bleeding and blisters and also purges. Dr. Dick, who at thirty-seven was by far the youngest of the three, argued that Washington was suffering from a 'violent inflammation of the membranes of the throat, which it had almost closed, and which if not immediately arrested, would result in death.' He urged an operation that would open the trachea below the infection so Washington could breathe…. Down the years doctors have speculated on the nature of Washington's illness. One guess is diphtheria, another a violent streptococcus infection of the throat. Either disease would, in the state of medicine at that time, have been fatal regardless of the treatment prescribed."[224]

Lear wrote of the last moments of George Washington. No other record survives. According to Lear, by ten o'clock that night, Washington spoke to him:

> "I am just going. Have me decently buried, and do not let my body be put into a vault in less than two days after I am dead."

Lear said Washington then looked directly at him:

"Do you understand me?" he commanded.

Lear responded: "Yes, Sir."

"'Tis well." said Washington.

According to Lear, Martha sat by the foot of the bed and Lear held the General's hand. Some find that hard to believe, given the immense love of Martha and George for one another. Common sense dictates that Martha would have been holding her husband's hand while Lear respectfully remained at the foot of the bed. Servants, doctors and others, according to Lear, stood near the door. Washington's breathing became easier as the hour passed ten. He lay quietly. Gently, Washington withdrew his hand to feel his own pulse. Suddenly, a change in the General's countenance occurred and his fingers slipped away from his wrist. Two elements, body and soul had been mysteriously united in one reality for 67 years; in the blink of an eye, the humanity of George Washington separated from his immortal soul. The General had surrendered his last command.

Lear continues: Martha calmly asked: "Is he gone?" Lear, choking with emotion nodded affirmatively. Devout Christian that she was, Martha knew that her husband had just been born into heaven.[225] "'Tis well." she said, echoing the General's last words. "All is over now. I have no more trials to pass through. I shall soon follow him."[226] And two years later she was reunited with her husband in the land of the spirits.

Martha Washington, George Washington's beloved and dedicated wife of forty years helped her husband in all his pursuits of excellence: she accompanied him to battle scenes, shared the exhilaration, exhaustion and discipline of his Presidency, and was hostess to constant throngs who filled Mount Vernon. She contributed most intimately to the General's accomplishments and inspired his aspirations. George and Martha Washington were spiritual giants who paved American culture with the highest ideals of married life. The purpose of her husband's life, and surely of her own, like all people, was to cooperate with the loving plan of Kind Providence for humanity.

History reflects the magnificence of Washington's spiritual journey. At his death, onlookers commented:

"Martha's fortitude reflected that of the General. The quietness with which he had borne his pain through the long day and she her sorrow made them the more poignant for those who merely watched and worked."[227]

George Washington was buried in the family vault at Mount Vernon thirteen days before the end of that tumultuous millennium, December 18, 1799. A solemn procession to the vault was led by cavalry, infantrymen and the guard, all with arms reversed, followed by the band, the clergy, and the General's horse. Four lieutenants of the Virginia militia carried the bier. Six honorary pall bearers marched, three on each side. Family, friends and dignitaries followed. Those who lived and worked on the Washington estates comprised the rest of the procession. The Minister, Reverend Davis read the Order of Burial from the Episcopal Prayer Book. Washington's rector gave a brief eulogy. When all was finished, minute guns from Robert Hamilton's schooner, anchored close by in the Potomac, fired their final salute to America's Founding Father. Eleven artillery cannon answered.

King William IV, son of George III of England, unabashedly declared George Washington the greatest man who ever lived. Congressman Light Horse Harry Lee of Virginia entered into the Congressional Record that Washington was "first in war, first in peace and first in the hearts of his countrymen."

Washington, true Son of the Republic in deed and spirit, looked and learned, served. He loved and died that America might always be one nation under God with liberty and justice for all.

Kind Providence was with George Washington. The great God of Abraham chose him as Founding Father of the United States. George Washington was faithful to the end of no end for he is immortal.

Afterword

Each true patriot will find threads of his or her own spiritual journey represented in the prophetic Farewell Address of George Washington. The challenge remains to move ahead in pursuit of the highest ideals of human munificence. Each generation bears a moral imperative to do so.

Excerpts From George Washington's
Farewell Address

United States, 19th September, 1796

Friends, & Fellow—Citizens.

… I will only say, that I have, with good intentions, contributed towards the Organization and Administration of the government, the best exertions of which a very fallible judgment was capable….

…my feelings do not permit me to suspend the deep acknowledgment of that debt of gratitude which I owe to my beloved country, for the many honors it has conferred upon me; still more for the steadfast confidence with which it has supported me; and for the opportunities I have thence enjoyed of manifesting my inviolable attachment, by services faithful & persevering, though in usefulness unequal to my zeal. If benefits have resulted to our country from these services, let it always be remembered to your praise, and as an instructive example in our annals, that, under circumstances in which the Passions agitated in every direction were liable to mislead, amidst appearances sometimes dubious, vicissitudes of fortune often discouraging, in situations in which not infrequently want of Success has countenanced the spirit of criticism, the constancy of your support was the essential prop of the efforts, and a guarantee of the plans by which they were effected. Profoundly penetrated with this idea, I shall carry it with me to my grave, as a strong incitement to unceasing vows that Heaven may continue to you the choicest tokens of its beneficence—that your Union & brotherly affection may be perpetual—that the free constitution, which is the work of your hands, may be sacredly maintained—that its Administration in every department may be stamped with wisdom and Virtue—that, in fine, the happiness of the people of these States, under the auspices of liberty, may be made complete, by so careful a preservation and so prudent a use of this blessing as will acquire to them the glory of recommending it to the applause, the affection—and adoption of every nation which is yet a stranger to it.

The Unity of Government which constitutes you one people is also now dear to you. It is justly so; for it is a main Pillar in the Edifice of your real independence, the support of your tranquility at home; your peace abroad; of your safety; of your prosperity; of that very Liberty which you so highly prize. But as it is easy to foresee, that from different causes & from different quarters, much pains will be taken, many artifices employed, to weaken in your minds the conviction of this truth; as this is the point in your political fortress against which the batteries of internal & external enemies will be most constantly and actively (though often covertly & insidiously) directed, it is of infinite moment, that you should properly estimate the immense value of your national Union to your collective & individual happiness; that you should cherish a cordial, habitual & immovable attachment to it; accustoming yourselves to think and speak of it as of the Palladium of your political safety and prosperity; watching for its preservation with jealous anxiety; discountenancing whatever may suggest even a suspicion that it can in any event be abandoned, and indignantly frowning upon the first dawning of every attempt to alienate any portion of our Country from the rest, or to enfeeble the sacred ties which now link together the various parts.

For this you have every inducement of sympathy and interest. Citizens by birth or choice, of a common country, that country has a right to concentrate your affections. The name of American, which belongs to you, in your national capacity, must always exalt the just pride of Patriotism, more than any appellation derived from local discriminations. With slight shades of difference, you have the same Religion, Manners, Habits & political Principles. You have in a common cause fought & triumphed together. The independence & liberty you possess are the work of joint councils, and joint efforts—of common dangers, sufferings and successes.

But these considerations, however powerfully they address themselves to your sensibility are greatly outweighed by those which apply more immediately to your Interest. Here every portion of our country finds the most commanding motives for carefully guarding & preserving the Union of the whole.

...[Y]our union ought to be considered as a main prop of your liberty, and that the love of the one ought to endear to you the preservation of the other.

...With such powerful and obvious motives to Union, affecting all parts of our country, while experience shall not have demonstrated its impracticability, there will always be reason, to distrust the patriotism of those, who in any quarter may endeavor to weaken its bands.

...Of all the dispositions and habits which lead to political prosperity, Religion and morality are indispensable supports. In vain would that man claim the tribute of Patriotism, who should labor to subvert these great Pillars of human happiness, these firmest props of the duties of Men & citizens. The mere Politician, equally with the pious man ought to respect & to cherish them. ....Whatever may be conceded to the influence of refined education on minds of peculiar structure—reason & experience both forbid us to expect that National morality can prevail in exclusion of religious principle.

...Observe good faith & justice towards all Nations. Cultivate peace & Religion & morality enjoin this conduct; and can it be that good policy does not equally enjoin it? It will be worthy of a free, enlightened, and, at no distant period, a great Nation, to give to mankind the magnanimous and too novel example of a People always guided by an exalted justice & benevolence.[228]

Finally

George Washington believed that people receive the power to live happy, prosperous and healthy lives from Almighty God, Kind Providence. Divine gifts, he warned, are reciprocal. He articulated the duty of all people in his Thanksgiving Proclamation, October 3, 1789.

> "...[I]t is the duty of all Nations to acknowledge the Providence of Almighty God, to obey His will, to be grateful for His benefits, and humbly to implore His protection and favor."[229]

Americans need never fear. Indomitable faith, trust in the merciful love of Kind Providence, adherence to the ways of Kind Providence, sacrificial service, gracious stewardship are George Washington's most enduring legacy. Kind Providence's grace is sufficient for all times.

Appendix I

The Declaration of Independence is a spiritual document that was startling in its day. After more than two hundred years, its contents brilliantly illumine the reality that people are made in the image of the Creator, a Kind Providence and naturally are entitled to dignity and respect. But for the spiritual journey of George Washington, the signers of the Declaration of Independence would have been condemned and executed as traitors. Such visionary courage is as immeasurable as it is indomitable.

The Declaration of Independence

When in the Course of human events, it becomes necessary for one people to dissolve the political bands which have connected them with another, and to assume among the powers of the earth, the separate and equal station to which the Laws of Nature and Nature's God entitle them, a decent respect to the opinions of mankind requires that they should declare the causes which impel them to the separation. —

We hold these truths to be self evident, that all men are created equal, that they are endowed by their Creator with certain unalienable Rights, that among these are Life, Liberty and the pursuit of Happiness. —

That to secure these rights, Governments are instituted among Men, deriving their just powers from the consent of the governed. —

That whenever any Form of Government becomes destructive of these ends, it is the Right of the People to alter or to abolish it, and to institute new Government, laying its foundation on such principles and organizing its powers in such form, as to them shall seem most likely to effect their Safety and Happiness. Prudence, indeed, will dictate that Governments long established should not be changed for light and transient causes; and accordingly all experience hath shewn, that man-kind are more disposed to suffer, while evils are sufferable, than to right themselves by abolishing the forms to which they are accustomed. But when a long train of abuses and usurpations, pursuing invariably the same Object evinces a design to reduce them under absolute Despotism, it is their right, their duty, to throw off such Government, and to provide new Guards for their future security. —

Such has been the patient suffering of these Colonies; and such is now the necessity which constrains them to alter their former Systems of Government. The history of the present King of Great Britain is a history of repeated injuries and usurpations, all having in direct object the establishment of an absolute Tyranny over these States. To prove this, let facts be submitted to a candid world. —

He has refused his Assent to Laws, the most wholesome and necessary for the public good. —

He has forbidden his Governors to pass Laws of immediate and pressing importance, unless suspended in their operation till his Assent should be obtained; and when so suspended, he has utterly neglected to attend to them. —

He has refused to pass other Laws for the accommodation of large districts of people, unless those people would relinquish the right of representation in the Legislature, a right inestimable to them and formidable to tyrants only. —

He has called together legislative bodies at places unusual, uncomfortable, and distant from the depository of their public Records, for the sole purpose of fatiguing them into compliance with his measures. —

He has dissolved Representative Houses repeatedly, for opposing with manly firmness his invasions on the rights of the people. —

He has refused for a long time, after such dissolutions, to cause others to be elected; whereby the Legislative powers, incapable of Annihilation, have returned to the People at large for their exercise; the State remaining in the mean time exposed to all the dangers of invasion from without, and convulsions within. —

He has endeavored to prevent the population of these States; for that purpose obstructing the Laws for Naturalization of Foreigners; refusing to pass others to encourage their migrations hither, and raising the conditions of new Appropriations of Lands. —

He has obstructed the Administration of Justice, by refusing his Assent to Laws for establishing Judiciary powers. —

He has made Judges dependent on his will alone, for the tenure of their offices, and the amount and payment of their salaries. —

He has erected a multitude of New Offices, and sent hither swarms of Officers to harass our people, and eat out their substance. —

He has kept among us, in times of peace, Standing Armies without the consent of our legislatures. —

He has effected to render the Military independent of and superior to the Civil power. —

He has combined with others to subject us to a jurisdiction foreign to our constitution, and acknowledged by our laws; giving his Assent to their Acts of pretended Legislation. —

For quartering large bodies of armed troops among us. —

For protecting them, by a mock Trial, from punishment for any Murders which they should commit on the Inhabitants of these States. —

For cutting off our Trade with all parts of the world: —

For imposing Taxes on us without our Consent: —

For depriving us in many cases, of the benefits of Trial by Jury: —

For transporting us beyond Seas to be tried for pretended offenses: —

For abolishing the free System of English Laws in a neighboring Province, establishing therein an Arbitrary government, and enlarging its Boundaries so as to render it at once an example and fit instrument for introducing the same absolute rule into these Colonies: —

For taking away our Charters, abolishing our most valuable laws, and altering fundamentally the Forms of our Governments: —

For suspending our own Legislatures, and declaring themselves invested with power to legislate for us in all cases whatsoever. —

He has abdicated Government here, by declaring us out of his Protection and waging War against us. —

He has plundered our seas, ravaged our Coasts, burnt our towns, and destroyed the lives of our people. —

He is at this time transporting large Armies of foreign Mercenaries to complete the works of death, desolation and tyranny, already begun with circumstances of Cruelty and perfidy scarcely paralleled in the most barbarous ages, and totally unworthy the Head of a civilized nation. —

He has constrained our fellow Citizens taken captive on the high Seas to bear Arms against their Country, to become the executioners of their friends and Brethren, or to fall themselves by their Hands. —

He has incited domestic insurrections amongst us, and has endeavored to bring on the inhabitants of our frontiers, the merciless Indian Savages, whose known rule of warfare, is an undistinguished destruction, of all ages, sexes and conditions.

In every stage of these Oppressions We have Petitioned for Redress in the most humble terms: Our repeated Petitions have been answered only by repeated injury. A prince, whose character is thus marked by every act which may define a Tyrant, is unfit to be the ruler of a free people.

Nor have we been wanting in attentions to our British brethren. We have warned them from time to time of attempts by their legislature to extend an unwarrantable jurisdiction over us. We have reminded them of the circumstances of our emigration and settlement here. We have appealed to their native justice and magnanimity, and we have conjured them by the ties of our common kindred to disavow these usurpation's, which, would inevitably interrupt our connections and correspondence. They too have been deaf to the voice of justice and consanguinity. We must, therefore, acquiesce in the necessity, which denounces our Separation, and hold them, as we hold the rest of mankind, Enemies in War, in Peace Friends. —

We, therefore, the Representatives of the United States of America, in General Congress, Assembled, appealing to the Supreme Judge of the world for the rectitude of our intentions, do, in the Name, and by Authority of the good People of these Colonies, solemnly publish and declare, That these United Colonies are, and of Right ought to be Free and Independent States; that they are Absolved from all Allegiance to the British Crown, and that all political connection between them and the State of Great Britain, is and ought to be totally dissolved; and that as Free and Independent States, they have full Power to levy War, conclude Peace, contract Alliances, establish Commerce, and do all other Acts and Things which Independent States may of right do. —

And for the support of this Declaration, with a firm reliance on the protection of divine Providence, we mutually pledge to each other our Lives, our Fortunes, and our sacred Honor.

Appendix II

*T*his prayer was recited by the congregation in all the services George Washington would have attended in his Anglican/Episcopalian faith tradition, and is continued to the present. It traces its origins to the Council of Constantinople in 381, and is the profession of the Christian faith of the Catholic Church and all Eastern Churches, as well as most Protestant denominations. As such, the prayer is the religious belief of George Washington.

The Nicene Creed

We believe in one God,
The Father, the Almighty,
Maker of heaven and earth,
And all that is seen and unseen.

We believe in one Lord, Jesus Christ,
the only Son of God,
eternally begotten of the Father,
God from God, Light from Light,
true God from true God,
begotten, not made, one in Being with the Father.
Through him all things were made.
For us men and for our salvation

he came down from heaven.

by the power of the Holy Spirit,
He was born of the Virgin Mary, and became man.

For our sake he was crucified under Pontius Pilot;
he suffered, died, and was buried.
on the third day he rose again
in fulfillment of the Scriptures;
he ascended in to heaven
and is seated at the right hand of the Father.
He will come again in glory to judge the living and the
dead,
And his kingdom will have no end.

We believe in the Holy Spirit, the Lord, the giver of life,
Who proceeds from the Father and the Son.
With the Father and the Son he is worshipped and glo-
rified.
He has spoken through the Prophets.
We believe in one holy catholic and apostolic Church.
We acknowledge one baptism for the forgiveness of sins.
We look for the resurrection of the dead,
and the life of the world to come. Amen.

Acknowledgments

*T*he reported apparition of Our Lady of Valley Forge sent me on the journey into the spiritual life of George Washington. Any good that comes from this book is totally attributable to Kind Providence.

Throughout the research on this book, many wonderful people who love their country, some of whom have chosen to remain anonymous, helped me. I am deeply grateful.

John Donovan and his colleagues at the Pentagon kept me at work on this book over the years. Thank you for all you do for our country.

U.S. troops demonstrate what true Americans are. None can thank them enough.

I especially thank Professor Thomas King, S.J., and the late Professor Paul Cioffi, S.J., Georgetown University, for the handed-down oral history of the sacramental death of George Washington. Special thanks to Professor Robert Faricy, S.J., for his disciplined guidance.

Theresa Martin, Margaret M. Heckler, Bill Hammond, the late Frederic Flach, M.D., Andrew Flach, Kevin Moran, and Andrea Au all contributed in many ways to this manuscript.

The Mount Vernon Ladies' Association, the University of Virginia Library, the National Park Service, and especially the Valley Forge Museum provided invaluable historical data and insights into the spirit of George Washington reflected in this book. Heartfelt thanks to each of you who work in hallowed historical places. You labor with heroic valor to preserve the facts and fruits of Washington's life for future generations and are deserving of great respect.

My appreciation is deep and lasting for George Washington's biographers and is matched only by my admiration.

My husband Edward's patience, wit and wisdom are reflected throughout this book. I am so very grateful. Our children and grandchildren, William and Regina Connell, Jessica and Christian, Ted and Jennifer Connell, Lilly and Teddy, Betsy and Derek Minno, Mary Christian and Derek Jr., are my great teachers. I thank God for them and pray they and all generations will have the immense privilege of living the American dream.

Selected Bibliography

Aikman, Lonnelle. *Rider with a Destiny: George Washington*. McLean, VA: Link Press Publishers, 1983.

Alden, John R. *George Washington, A Biography*. Baton Rough, LA: Louisiana State University Press, 1884.

Anderson, Fred. *The War That Made America*. New York, The Penguin Group, 2005.

Bradford, M.E. *Founding Fathers*. 2d ed. Lawrence, KS: University Press of Kansas, 1981.

Bruns, Roger. *George Washington*. Philadelphia: Chelsea House Publishers, 1987.

Burk, Herbert W. *Washington's Prayers*. Norristown, PA. Published for the Benefit of the Washington Memorial Chapel, 1907.

Clark, Harrison. *All Cloudless Glory. 2 vols. The Life of George Washington: Making a Nation*. Washington, DC: Regnery Publications, Inc., 1995.

Ellis, Joseph J. *Founding Brothers*. New York: Vintage Books, 2000.

————. *His Excellency George Washington*. New York: Alfred A. Knopf, 2004.

Ferling, John. *Setting the World Ablaze*. New York: Oxford University Press, 2000.

Fields, Joseph E. *The Life of Martha Washington*. Westport, CT: Greenwood Press, 1994.

Flexner, James Thomas. *Washington The Indispensable Man*. Boston: Little, Brown and Company, 1969.

Freeman, Douglas Southall. *Washington*. With New Introduction by Michael Kammen, Afterword by Dumas Malone. An Abridgment by Richard Harwell. New York: Touchstone, 1968.

Gregg, Gary L. and Matthew Spalding, eds. *Patriot Sage: George Washington and the American Political Tradition*. Wilmington, Delaware: ISI Books, 1999.

Hanley, Thomas O'Brien. *Charles Carroll of Carrollton*. Chicago: Loyola University Press. 1982.

Hawke, David Freeman. *Everyday Life in Early America*. New York: Harper & Row, 1988.

Higginbotham, Don. *The War of American Independence: Military Attitudes, Policies, and Practice, 1763–1789*. New York: MacMillan, 1971.

Holmes, David L. *The Faiths of the Founding Fathers*. New York: Oxford University Press, 2006.

Johnson, Gerald W. *Mount Vernon: The Story of a Shrine*. Mount Vernon, VA: Mount Vernon Ladies Association, 1991.

Johnson, William J. *George Washington, The Christian*. Arlington, Texas: Christian Liberty Press, 1919.

Lambert, Frank. *The Founding Fathers and the Place of Religion in America*. Princeton: Princeton University Press, 2003.

Langguth, A.J. *Patriots: the Men Who Started the American Revolution*. New York: Simon & Schuster, 1988.

Lucas, Stephen E. ed. *The Quotable George Washington*. Madison, Wisconsin: Madison House Publishers, Inc., 1999.

Marshall, John. *The Life of George Washington. 4 vols.* Elibron Classic Series. Philadelphia: Adamant Media Corporation, 2005.

McCullaugh, David. *John Adams*. NY: Simon & Schuster, 2001.
———. *1776*. New York: Simon & Schuster, 2006.

McDonald, Forest. *The Presidency of George Washington*. Lawrence: University Press of Kansas, 1974.

McGuire, E.C., ed. *The Religious Opinions of Washington*. New York: Harper & Brothers, 1836.

Meacham, Jon. *American Gospel*, New York: Random House, 2006.

Morison, Samuel Eliot, Henry Steele Commager; and William Leuchtenburg, eds. *A Concise History of the American Republic*. New York: Oxford University Press, 1958.

Morison, Samuel Eliot, and Henry Steele Commager. *The Growth of the American Republic*, 2 vols. New York: Oxford University Press, 1958.

Needleman, Jacob. *The American Soul*. New York: Jeremy P. Tharcher/Putnam, 2002.

Novak, Michael. *On Two Wings*. San Francisco: Encounter Books, 2002.

Novak, Michael and Jana Novak. *Washington's God*. New York: Basic Books, 2006.

Phillips, John T., ed. *George Washington. Rules of Civility*. Leesburg, VA: Goose Creek Productions, 2000.

Schroeder, John Frederick. *Gerald R. Ford, Introduction, Maxims of George Washington*. Mount Vernon, VA: Mount Vernon Ladies Society, 1989.

Sharp, James Roger. *American Politics in the Early Republic: The New Nation in Crisis*. New Haven CT: Yale University Press, 1993.

Shy, John. *A People Numerous and Armed: Reflections on the Military Struggle for American Independence*. Ann Arbor: University of Michigan Press, 1990.

Sparks, Jared, ed. 12 vols. *The Writings of George Washington*. Boston: Ferdinand Andrews Publisher, 1838.

Tuchman, Barbara. *The First Salute*. New York: Knopf, 1988.

Twohig, Dorothy. ed. *George Washington's Diaries*. Charlottesville and London: University Press of Virginia, 1999.

Ward, Christopher. *The War of the Revolution*. Vols. 1 and 11. New York: Macmillan, 1952.

Wills, Gary. *Cincinnatus: George Washington and the Enlightenment*. Garden City, NY: Doubleday, 1984.

Notes

[1]Letter to Richard Henderson, June 19, 1788, *George Washington, Writings*, Volume 29, p. 520, as quoted in *Maxims of George Washington*, collected and arranged by John Frederick Schroeder, (ed.) Mount Vernon, VA: The Mount Vernon Ladies' Association, 1989, p. 51.

[2]Washington's Letter to John Adams, April 15, 1776, Washington's Letter to Benjamin Franklin, May 20, 1776. Washington addressed God as "Kind Providence" in seven additional writings, the last to John Adams, the President of the United States, July 13, 1798, one year before Washington's death. Obviously, Washington's vast life experience continued to reinforce his understanding of God as "Kind Providence."

[3]Mt. 7:7,8.

[4]To the Legislature of New Jersey, December 6, 1783.

[5]See Chapter Three, *supra*.

[6]To the Inhabitants of Canada, September 1775.

[7]To the Secretary of War, November 17, 1799.

[8]See Chapter Seven, *supra.*

[9]Answer to an Address from the Massachusetts Legislature, March 28, 1776.

[10]Letter to Governor Jonathan Trumbull, April 15, 1784.

[11]General Orders, February 27, 1776.

[12]Circular to the States, June 8, 1783.

[13]Washington to Nathanial Greene, February 6, 1783, as quoted in Joseph J. Ellis, *His Excellency George Washington,* New York: Alfred A. Knopf, 2004, p. 111.

[14]Ellis, *op. cit.,* p. xiv.

[15]Michael Novak and Jana Novak, *Washington's God,* New York: Basic Books, 2006, p. 224.

[16]David McCullough, *1776,* New York: Simon & Schuster, 2005, p. 289.

[17]John R. Alden, *George Washington, A Biography,* Baton Rouge, LA: Louisiana State University Press, 1984, p. 25.

[18]*Diaries* 1:127-28, as quoted in Ellis, *op. cit.,* p. 3.

[19]Alden, *op. cit.,* p. 27.

[20]*Ibid.*, p. 29.

[21]Letter to Governor Dinwiddie, *Writings*, Volume 1, p. 300, as quoted in Schroeder, *op. cit.*, p. 110.

[22]*Writings*, Volume 1, p. 325, as quoted in Schroeder, *op. cit.*, p. 123.

[23]*Diaries* 1:153-57, as quoted in Ellis, *op. cit.*, p. 4.

[24]Ellis, *op. cit.*, p. 6. The record is unclear just why Washington inherited this "Indian title."

[25]*Diaries* 1:36-40. As quoted in Ellis, *op. cit.*, p. 6.

[26]*Writings*, Volume 4, p. 483.

[27]Jon Meacham, *American Gospel*, New York: Random House. 2006, p. 19.

[28]*Ibid.*, pp. 19-20.

[29]*Ibid.*, p. 20.

[30]To the Inhabitants of the Island of Bermuda, September 6, 1775.

[31]Thanksgiving Proclamation, October 3, 1789.

[32]To Annis Boudinot Stockton, August 31, 1788.

[33]To the Ministers, Elders, Deacons, and Members of the Reformed German Congregation of New York, November 27, 1783.

[34]First Inaugural Address, April 30, 1789.

[35]Washington's letter to Bartholomew Dandridge, Philadelphia, March 8, 1797, as quoted in Stephen E. Lucas, (ed.), *The Quotable George Washington*, Madison, Wisconsin: Madison House, 1999, p. 50.

[36]M.E. Bradford, *Founding Fathers*, Lawrence, KS: University Press of Kansas, 1982, p. 126.

[37]David L. Holmes, *Faiths of the Founding Fathers*, New York: Oxford University Press, 2006, p. 13.

[38]Samuel Eliot Morison and Henry Steele Commager, *Growth of the American Republic*, Volume 1, New York: Oxford University Press, 1958, p. 51.

[39]Holmes, *op. cit.*, p. 34

[40]*Ibid.*, p. 35.

[41]Morison and Commager, *op. cit.*, p. 51.

[42]*Ibid.*, p. 33.

[43]Novak and Novak, *op. cit.*, p. 18.

[44]*Ibid.*, p. 9 quoting Mason Locke Weems, *A History of the Life, Death, Virtues, and Exploits of George Washington*, Philadelphia: Lippencott, 1918. See also Novak and Novak, *op. cit.*, Note 11, Chapter 1.

[45]Douglas Southall Freeman, *Washington*, New York: Touchstone, 1968, p. 4.

[46]Novak and Novak, *op. cit.*, p. 7.

[47]Rule 110 of the *Rules of Civility*.

[48]John T. Phillips, *George Washington's Rules of Civility*, Leesburg, VA: Goosecreek Productions, 2000, p. 7.

[49]Rev. Marye was born and raised in Rouen, France. He studied for and was ordained to the priesthood in the Jesuit College of Rouen. In 1726, he fled to England and became an Anglican priest.

[50]*The Rules of Civility and Decent Behavior in Company and Conversation, ca 1744,* are available on the Internet at http://www.history.org/Almanack/life/manners/rules2.cfm, among other sites. (Accessed 15 May 2007).

[51]Gary L. Gregg and Matthew Spalding (eds.), *Patriot Sage*, Wilmington, DE: ISI Books, 1999, quoting Richard Brookhiser, Afterword, p. 302.

[52]Letter from Abigail Adams to her sister Mary Smith Cranch, December 22, 1799, Philadelphia, quoted in Peter Hannaford, *The Essential George Washington: Two Hundred Years of Observations on the Man, the Myth, the Patriot*, Bennington, VT.: Images from the Past, 1999, pp. 5-6.

[53]Gregg and Spalding (eds.), *op. cit.*, quoting Richard Brookhiser, Afterword, pp. 303-304.

[54]From a letter to Martha Custis, his fiancée, by George Washington written from Fort Cumberland, July 20, 1758.

[55]Meacham, *op. cit.*, pp. 22-23.

[56]William J. Johnson, *George Washington the Christian*, Arlington, Texas: Christian Liberty Press, 1919, quoting Washington's heir's attestation, p. 242-245.

[57]Johnson, *op. cit.*, p. 23.

[58]Tim LaHaye, *Faith of Our Founding Fathers*, Green Forest, Arkansas: Master Books, Inc., 1990, p. 110.

[59]"Father of All Mercies" To the Hebrew Congregation of Newport, Rhode Island, August 18, 1790.

[60]John 15:21.

[61]Prov. 1:7.

[62]LaHaye, *op. cit.*, p. 108.

[63]See Appendix II.

[64]A title given to George Washington by Pulitzer Prize winning author Joseph J. Ellis.

[65]Some dispute authenticity because there are no spelling errors in the manuscript, though Washington often made spelling errors. Perhaps he put more effort into this manuscript, given the sacred nature of the assignment. With advances in technology, and the global interest in the subject, it is hoped that a conclusive assessment of authenticity will be forthcoming.

[66]See page 61, *supra*.

[67]Letter to George Steptoe Washington, Philadelphia, December 5, 1790, as quoted in Lucas, (ed.), *op. cit.*, p. 14.

[68]Peter H. Henriques, Ph.D., *George Washington America's First President*, National Park Services: Eastern National Publisher, 2002, p. 5

[69]Freeman, *op. cit.*, pp 18-19.

[70]Bradford, *op. cit.*, p. 127.

[71]A life interest that would end at the death of his widow should she survive him, or at his death if he had no spouse at the time of his death.

[72]Although 29 of the 56 signers of the Declaration of Independence were graduates of Colonial or British Institutes of higher learning, Washington was not.

[73]Morison and Commager, *op, cit.,* p. 113.

[74]*Diaries,* December 15, 1753, as quoted in Lonnnelle Aikman, *Rider with a Destiny,* George Washington, McLean, VA: Link Press, 1983, pp. 18-20.

[75]*Ibid.*

[76]Those left behind in the wagons were slaughtered during the battle.

[77]George Washington's letter to his brother John A. Washington, July 18, 1755.

[78]Freeman, *op. cit.,* p. 86.

[79]Washington as quoted in Morrison and Commager, *op. cit.,* p. 123.

[80]Bradford, *op. cit.,* p. 127.

[81]Aikman, *op. cit.,* p. 23. See also James Thomas Flexner,

Washington, The Indispensable Man, New York: New American Library, 1979, pp. 34, 35 and Freeman, *op. cit.*, pp. 133, 134.

[82]Henriques, *op. cit.*, p. 13.

[83]*Ibid.*, p. 13.

[84]Johnson, *op. cit.*, pp. 41-42. See also George Washington Parke Curtis, *The Indian Prophesy: A National Drama in Two Acts Founded Upon a Most Interesting and Romantic Occurrence in the Life of General Washington*, New York: Kessinger Publishing, 2005.

[85]Letter to Thaddeus Kosciuszko, August 31, 1797, *Writings*, p. 22, as quoted in Schroeder (ed.), *op. cit.*, p. 177.

[86]John Ferling, *Setting the World Ablaze*, New York: Oxford University Press, 2000, p. 8, quoting Rosemarie Zagarri, (ed.). *David Humphreys' Life of General Washington with George Washington's "Remarks"*, Athens, GA: University of Georgia Press, 1991, pp. xiii, xx, 5-6.

[87]*Ibid*, p. 9, quoting George Washington Parke Custis, *Recollections and Private Memories of Washington*, New York, 1860, 131, footnote 20, p. 312.

[88]*Ibid.*, p. 10.

[89]*Ibid.*, p. xiv.

[90]Fred Anderson, *The War That Made America*, New York: The Penguin Group, 2005, pp. 261-262.

[91]Gregg and Spalding (eds.), *op. cit.,* p. 186, quoting Marvin Olasky, *The American Leadership Tradition: Moral Vision From Washington to Clinton*, New York: The Free Press, 1999, p. 17.

[92]Ellis, *op. cit.*, p. 113.

[93]*Ibid.*

[94]*Ibid.*, p. 113.

[95]*Ibid.*

[96]*Ibid.*, p. 114.

[97]Bradford quoting Flexner, *op. cit.*, p. 129.

[98]Flexner, *op. cit.*, p. xvi.

[99]Bradford, *op. cit.*, p. 129.

[100]Alden, *op. cit.*, pp. 103, 112.

[101]Quoted in Gregg and Spalding (eds.), *op. cit.*, p. 186.

[102]Bradford, *op. cit.*, p. 133.

[103]*Writings*, XI: 342-343, General Orders of 5/2/1778, as quoted in Johnson, *op. cit.*, p. 112.

[104]Barbara W. Tuchman, *The First Salute*, New York: Knopf, 1988, p. 183.

[105]*Writings*, Volume 11, p. 291.

[106]Matthew 6:5.

[107]Matthew 6:6. As quoted by George Washington's step-granddaughter, Nelly Custis Lewis, sharing her eyewitness observations of George Washington's prayer life with Harvard historian Jared Sparks.

[108]William J. Bennett, *Our Sacred Honor*, Nashville, Tennessee: Broadman & Holman Publishers, 1997, p. 378.

[109]George Washington's letter to his captains on the frontier in 1757.

[110]Washington's First Inaugural Address, April 30, 1789.

[111]Jay Tolson, *U.S. News and World Report*, September 2000, p. 14.

[112]Painting of the event in the Grainger Collection, New York and reproduced in Meacham, *op. cit.*, p. 15.

[113]Holmes, *op. cit.*, p. 70.

[114]George Washington, The Circular Address to the States, June 8, 1783.

[115]Ferling, *op. cit.*, pp. 265-266.

[116]George Washington Parke Custis, *Recollections and Private Memoirs of Washington*, p. 493.

[117]Jacob Needleman, *The American Soul*, New York: Penquin Putnam, 2002, p. 109.

[118]George Washington's letter to Edward Newenham, October 20, 1792.

[119]George Washington's letter to Francis Adrian Van der Kemp, Mennonite minister, May 28, 1788.

[120]Needleman, *op. cit.*, pp. 106-107.

[121]Washington's Address to the Continental Army before the Battle of Long Island, August 27, 1776, as quoted in Johnson, *op. cit.*, p. 82.

[122]Letter of March 15, 1790, *Writings*, Volume 31, p. 22, as quoted in Schroeder (ed.), *op. cit.*, p. 179.

[123]New York, May 1789, as quoted in Lucas, *op. cit.*, p. 81 and in W.B. Allen (ed.), *George Washington: A Collection*, Indianapolis: Liberty Fund, 1988, pp. 533-534.

124Allen, *op. cit.*, p. 533.

125Freeman, *op. cit.*, p. 585.

126Union General William Tecumseh Sherman said these words during the Civil War.

127Novak and Novak, *op. cit.*, p. 130.

128*Ibid.*, p. xiv.

129Alden, *op. cit.*, p. 12.

130Novak and Novak, *op. cit.*, p. 12.

131Johnson, *op. cit.*, p. 198.

132Thomas Nelson, Jr., Esquire, 1738-1789, was a member of the house of burgesses in 1774 and was appointed to the first general convention which net at Williamsburg on the first of August of that year. In 1775 he was appointed a Virginia delegate to the continental congress in Philadelphia. He served as a brigadier general and com-mander-in-chief of the forces of the commonwealth of Virginia. In 1781, he became Governor of Virginia. He was greatly admired by General George Washington, who in his general orders of the 20th of October, 1781 said of him: "The general [Washington] would be guilty of the highest ingratitude if he forgot to return his sincere acknowledge-ments to his Excellency Governor Nelson, for the succors which he received from him, and the militia under his command, to whose activity, emulation, and bravery, the highest praises are due." As quoted in Rev. Charles A. Goodrich, *Lives of the Signers of the Declaration of Independence*, William Reed & Co., 1856, pp. 410-415.

[133]Freeman, *op. cit.*, p. xxiv.

[134]At a meeting at the City Tavern in Georgetown, when provisions for the Society of the Cincinnati were being formulated, Washington became first President-General. He expected that the Society of the Cincinnati be created to care for his troops, their widows and children. He insisted that the delegates to the Society 'strike out every word, sentence and clause which has a political tendency'. See Freeman, *op. cit.*, p. 520.

[135]Aikman, *op. cit.*, p. 70.

[136]Chief Justice John Marshall as quoted in Freeman, *op. cit.*, p. xxiv.

[137]Freeman, *op. cit.*, p. 100.

[138]George Washington, Letter to Colonel Benedict Arnold, September 14, 1775.

[139]*Ibid.*

[140]Freeman, *op. cit.*, p. 39.

141 *Ibid.*, p. 41.

142 *Ibid.*, p. 56.

143 Allen, *op. cit.*, p. 549.

144 "Do unto others as you would have them do unto you."

145 Frank Lambert. *The Founding Fathers and the Place of Religion in America*, Princeton: Princeton University Press, 2003, p. 3.

146 Schroeder (ed.), *op. cit.*, p. 178.

147 George Washington letter to Samuel Langdon, September 28, 1789.

148 Alden, *op. cit.*, p. 146.

149 *Ibid.*, p. 149.

150 Quoting Forrest McDonald in Gregg and Spalding (eds.), *op. cit.*, pp. 25, 26.

151 Washington's letter to Secretary of State, July 29, 1795, as he was recalled to military duty. As quoted in Schroeder (ed.), *op. cit.*, p. 142.

152 Dickinson and Jefferson: Declaration of the Causes and Necessity of Taking Up Arms.

153 In the Mount Vernon collection is a document in Washington's handwriting in which he carefully kept account of his out-of-pocket expenses, and specifically Martha Washington's traveling expenses to and from his quarters during the war years.

154 Washington letter to Reverend Jonathan Boucher, December 16, 1777.

155 *Ibid.*

156 Washington's letter to his wife, June 18, 1775.

157 Washington had been heard to say of the British Parliament: "[T]hey have no more right to put their hands into my pocket, without my consent, than I have to put my hands into yours for money." As quoted in Bradford, *op. cit.*, p. 128.

158 Washington's letter to Martha Washington, June 18, 1775.

159 Attestation of Nelly Custis-Lewis, step granddaughter of George Washington to Harvard historian Jared Sparks.

160 *Ibid.*

161 Less faith-filled colonists of means, believing the cause of independence was lost, were forging personal alliances in the salons of Philadelphia with British diplomats. Many less committed colonists returned to England to live.

[162]See information at Valley Forge Museum concerning Washington during these six days at Valley Forge, PA.

[163]*The National Tribune*, Volume 4, No. 12, December 1880.

[164]Certain historical data about this purported apparition offered *verbatim* comes from data supplied by the Library of Congress Historical Research Department through the kindness of the Honorable Margaret M. Heckler.

[165]Janice T. Connell, *Angel Power*, New York: Ballantine, 1995, p. 217.

[166]St. Cyril of Alexandria (376-444). (See Appendix II, *supra.*)

[167]Signer of the Declaration of Independence on behalf of the State of Maryland.

[168]Woodstock Letters, *Reflections*, Volume 13, 1884. Courtesy of Rev. Thomas King, S.J., Department of Theology, Georgetown University, Washington, DC, reveals the familial friendship between Archbishop John Carroll and General Washington.

[169]*Ibid.*, p. 388.

[170]From the Basilica of the National Shrine of the Assumption of the Blessed Virgin Mary, Baltimore, MD.

[171]"The Old Testament theophanies of God in human form radiate from the ontological mystery of the Incarnation and the Theotokas in the New Testament. The Incarnation is the cause of creation and the source of all revelation. ...Without a human form, ...He could not be known....Because of the Mother of God, saints and angels were able to speak with God, 'mouth to mouth' [seeing Him] in a form and not in riddles." Num. 12: 8. As quoted in George S. Gabriel, *Mary The Untrodden Portal of God*, Ridgewood, NJ: Zephyr Publishing. 2000, p. 119. Courtesy of the Hon. Rev. Victor Potopov.

[172]*Ibid.*, p. 24.

[173]Janice T. Connell, *Meetings with Mary*, New York: Random House, 1995.

[174]Though the source of this oral history is more remote than absolute credibility would desire, it is more substantial than similar purported apparitions surrounding the founding of nation states, religious orders and global movements. See data regarding such apparitions is available at the National Shrine of the Immaculate Conception, Washington, DC.

[175]Thomas O'Brien Hanley, Charles Carroll of Carrolltown, *The Making of A Revolutionary Gentleman*, Chicago: Loyola University Press, 1982, p. 153.

[176]Morison and Commager, *op. cit.*, p. 221.

[177] *Ibid.*, p. 223.

[178] *Ibid.*

[179] George Washington's letter to Marquis de Lafayette, June 19, 1788, *George Washington, Writings*, Volume 29, p. 526 as quoted in Schroeder (ed.), *op. cit.*, p. 51.

[180] Jefferson's letter to John Adams, October 28, 1813.

[181] Jefferson's letter to Dr. Benjamin Rush, September 23, 1800.

[182] Alden, *op. cit.*, p. 80.

[183] *Ibid.*, p. 79.

[184] Joseph E. Fields, *Worthy Partner*, Westport, CT: Greenwood Press, 1994, p. ix.

[185] *Ibid.*

[186] Wendell Garrett, *George Washington's Mount Vernon*, New York: Menacelli Press, 1990, p. 24-26.

[187] Aikman, *op. cit.*, p. 144

[188] Alden, *op. cit.*, p. 82.

[189] *Ibid.*

[190]*Ibid.*, p. 83.

[191]*Ibid.*

[192]Letter to John Christian Ehler, Philadelphia, December 23, 1793.

[193]Johnson, *op. cit.*, p. 158.

[194]Morison and Commager, *op. cit.*, p. 18.

[195]Alden, *op. cit.*, p. 81.

[196]Genesis 12:1-4.

[197]Lambert, *op. cit.*, p. 240.

[198]*The Boston Price-Current and Marine Intelligencer*, June 26, 1797, as quoted in Lambert, *op. cit.*, pp. 238-239.

[199]Washington's letter to Henry Knox, Mount Vernon, April 1, 1789.

[200]Letter of George Washington to Tobias Lear, July 31, 1797.

[201]Hanley, *op. cit.*, p. 150.

[202]*Ibid.*, p. 152.

[203]Bradford, *op. cit.*, p. 125.

[204]As quoted in Freeman, *op. cit.*, p 740.

[205]*Ibid.*, p. 745.

[206]Johnson, *op. cit.*, pp. 231-232.

[207]As quoted in Freeman, *op. cit.*, p. 748.

[208]Meacham, *op. cit.*, p. 13, quoting biographer Patricia Brady.

[209]Novak and Novak, *op. cit.*, p. 15.

[210]Freeman, *op. cit.*, p. 715

[211]Ellis, *op. cit.*, p. 163.

[212]Johnson, *op. cit.*, pp. 226-227, quoting Elizabeth Bryant Johnson, *George Washington Day By Day*, 1894.

[213]Roger Burnes, *George Washington*, New York: Chelsea House Publishers, 1987, p. 109.

[214]*Ibid.*, p. 110.

[215]Dorothy Twohig (ed.), *George Washington's Diaries, An Abridgment*, Charlottesville and London: University Press of Virginia, 1999, pp. 428-431.

[216]Holmes, *op. cit.*, pp. 113-114.

[217]Freeman, *op. cit.*, p. 749.

[218]Alden, *op. cit.*, p. 303.

[219]Ellis, *op. cit.*, p. 268.

[220]*Ibid.*, p. 269.

[221]Freeman, *op. cit.*, p. 751.

[222]Prov. 8:31.

[223]For further information, contact Rev. Thomas King, S.J., Georgetown University, Washington, DC. Reference the archives of the Society of Jesus at Wernersville, MD. Volume 20, 1893, p. 498. See also Twohig, (ed.), *op. cit.*, p. 425, regarding June 11 entry.

[224]Flexner, *op. cit.*, pp. 399-400.

[225]John 16:20-23.

[226]Fields, *op. cit.*, p. xxvii.

[227]Freeman, *op. cit.*, p. 752.

[228]Two hundred four years after George Washington's Farewell Address, his ideals were yet again anthropomor-

phized: on April 12, 2003, Gerard Baker of the International Financial Times Limited said in his Comment and Analysis article entitled "The Land of the Free Enjoys the Thrill of Being a Force for Good": "It is this self-faith as much as anything that defines and differentiates Americans from most of the rest of the world. …Americans, almost alone in the world, have a serious, unironic, uncynical, even simplistic belief that their country is a force for enduring good. They acknowledge it does not always get it right, that at times its antics fall far short of its highest ideals, but all but the most hardened cynics really believe in America as a force for freedom and prosperity and in the universality of these goals. This belief is born of the country's history, religion and culture…. For most of the rest of the world, this ingenious faith in the nation's unyielding will and power to produce beneficial outcomes for everybody is almost non-existent…. But you can hardly blame Americans…for thinking that they sit on the right side of history. And you surely cannot help but marvel at the fact that they are almost alone in seeing themselves that way."

[229]George Washington's Thanksgiving Proclamation, October 3, 1789, as quoted in Schroeder (ed.), *op. cit.*, p. 172.

Illustration Credits

1 Photograph No. NWDNS-148-GW-46; "Washington, George, the Virginia Colonel," 1772; George Washington Bicentennial Commission, Record Group 148; National Archives at College Park, College Park, MD.

2 "Life of George Washington—The Citizen;" Junius Brutus Stears, artist; Library of Congress, Prints and Photography Division [LC-USZ62-3914].

3 "Mount Vernon in Virginia;" Francis Jukes, engraver; Library of Congress, Prints and Photography Division [LC-USZ62-1237].

4 Photograph No. NWDNS-148-GW-1141; "Reading of the Declaration of Independence from the East balcony of the Old State House, Boston, Massachusetts July 18, 1776," Copy of artwork, 1931-1932; George Washington Bicentennial Commission, Record Group 148; National Archives at College Park, College Park, MD.

5 Photograph No. NWDNS-148-GW-571; "Washington Taking Command of the American

Army, at Cambridge, Massachusetts July 3rd, 1775," Copy of Lithograph by Currier & Ives, 1876; George Washington Bicentennial Commission, Record Group 148; National Archives at College Park, College Park, MD.

6   Photograph   No.   NWDNS-148-GW-580; **"Washington at the Battle of Trenton. Decemeber 1776,"** Copy of engraving by Illman Brothers after E. L. Henry, circa 1870; George Washington Bicentennial Commission, Record Group 148; National Archives at College Park, College Park, MD.

7   Photograph   No.   NWDNS-148-GW-189; **"Valley Forge-Washington & Lafayette. Winter 1777-78,"** Copy of engraving by H.B. Hall after Alonzo Chappel, 1931-1932; George Washington Bicentennial Commission, Record Group 148; National Archives at College Park, College Park, MD.

8   Photograph No. NWDNS-148-GW-201; **"The Prayer at Valley Forge. General George Washington, winter 1777-78."** Copy of engraving by John C. McRae after Henry Brueckner, published 1866; George Washington Bicentennial Commission, Record Group 148; National Archives at College Park, College Park, MD.

Index